S0-BTB-499

How Detroit Changed History

How Detroit Changed History

Nelson Bolan

Brunswick

International Standard Book Number
1-55618-018-7

Library of Congress Catalog Card Number
87-70325

First Original Edition

Published in the United States of America

by

Brunswick Publishing Company
RT. 1, BOX 1A1
LAWRENCEVILLE, VIRGINIA 23868

Dedication

Dedicated to my wife, and all the others, who, while not understanding, have tolerated my fascination and appreciation of automobiles.

Contents

Introduction 3

The Mid 1890's 13
    The Beginning Of A New Industry
    The Ideal Car Size

1896 15
    Bicycles Greatly Improved
    King, Then Ford Each Drive Cars In Detroit
    Famous Bicycle Maker Begins Auto Manufacture
    Charles Ainsley Becomes Detroit's First Used-Car Buyer
    The Stanley's Get Serious

1897 20
    Mr. Packard Doesn't Like His New Winton Car
    Studebaker Looks Into The Automobile Idea
    The Olds Motor Works Comes Into Existence
    Rambler Experimental Car Is Completed

1898 22
    The Stanley's Sell Out To Eastman Kodak

1899 22
    The Stanley's Get An Offer They Can't Resist
    The President Goes For A Silent Ride

1900 25
    Locomobile Switches To Gasoline Power
    Mr. Packard Builds His First Car
    Auto Show Held In New York City
    Popular President Re-Elected

1901 25
    Oil Discovered In Texas
    Olds Fire A Blessing In Disguise
    David Buick's Life Starts Downhill
    Henry Ford Goes Into Business For The Second Time
    Roy Chapin Shows That Olds Has Recovered From Its Fire
    The Stanley's Start Over Again

1902 28
    How The "Cadillac" Car Came Into Being
    "Rambler" And "Studebaker" Cars Appear
    Henry Ford Makes One Of His Wisest Employment Decisions
    The Buick Company Is Floundering
    Two Automobile "Old Timers" Get Together

1903 34
    Cadillac, Buick, And Ford Make Modest Beginnings
    David Buick And Henry Ford Comparisons
    The Dusenberg Name First Appears In The Auto Business
    Packard Moves From Warren, Ohio To Detroit
    The Panama Canal Is Begun
    Orville And Wilbur Quietly Succeed Before Christmas

1904 44
    Mr. Olds Leaves The Olds Motor Works
    Henry Leland Joins Cadillac Full Time
    Studebaker Joins With Garford
    Buick Calls On W. C. Durant For Help
    The Hot Dog Becomes Popular

1905 48
    Cadillac And Ford No Longer Look Identical
    Durant Expands The Buick Facilities
    Henry Ford Buys Out One Of His Backers
    Dodge's Still Making Parts For Ford
    Ransom Olds Making Cars Again
    Henry Leland's Last New Car
    Swiss Born Louis Chevrolet Comes To The U.S.A.
    Walter Chrysler Still In Railroading
    Charles Nash Still In The Carriage Business
    Charles Kettering Makes National Cash Register Famous
    Roy Chapin Leaves Oldsmobile For Other Ventures

1906 53
    An Extremely Close Call For Roy Chapin And His Sister
    C. H. Wills Of Ford Motor Co. Makes Metallurgy Breakthrough
    British "Dewar Cup" Awarded To The Stanley

1907 57
    Ford Has Six Cylinder Engine Problems
    Henry Leland Brings Even More Precision To Cadillac
    J. P. Morgan And The Financial Panic Of 1907
    Fred Marriott Returns To Ormond Beach With The Stanley Racer

1908 61
    David Buick Leaves The Buick Motor Co.
    Walter Chrysler Buys His First Car
    Louis Chevrolet Goes To Work For The Buick Motor Co.
    Another Industry Develops Pressed Steel
    Roy Chapin Woos Hugh Chalmers From National Cash Register
    Dr. Hills Sells The First Buick
    General Motors Is Secretly Formed
    British "Dewar Trophy" Awarded To Cadillac

1909 73
    Oakland Joins General Motors
    General Motors Finally Buys Cadillac
    Model "T" Ford Brakes And Steering Explained
    Henry Ford Loses An Early Law Suit
    Roy Chapin And Friends Form The Hudson Motor Car Co.
    C. Y. Knight's Engine Helps British Firm Win Dewar Trophy

1910 79
    Kettering's Genius Solves An Early Problem
    The Impulse Buying Of Durant Breaks G.M.
    Mr. Durant And Mr. Ford Compared
    The Dodge Brothers Make Long Range Plans

1911 86
    Henry Ford Finds A Way To Keep His Name In The News Free
    Arthur Chevrolet Breaks Down At "Indy"
    Walter Chrysler Joins Buick And General Motors
    Durant Forms The Chevrolet Motor Co.
    Front Doors Begin Appearing On New Cars

1912 92
    The Starter Is Here To Stay
    Studebaker Absorbs E.M.F. To Save Face
    Walter Chrysler And Charles Nash Promoted By G.M.
    Bankers Influence In The Auto Industry
    Dr. Diesel's Personal Tragedy

1913 98
    Ford Adopts The Assembly Line To Auto Making
    U.S. Motors Folds And Maxwell Emerges
    Louis Chevrolet Leaves The Chevrolet Motor Co.
    Graduated Tax Is Law Despite The Constitution

1914 102
    Ford Pulls The Biggest Publicity Stunt Of All Time!
    Dodge's Form Their Own Company To Make Complete Cars
    Walter Chrysler Modernizes The Cars From Buick
    Durant Gets Financing For Chevrolet Production
    Cadillac Has A Patent Problem
    Maxwell Hires A Famous Racing Driver
    The Austrian Archduke Is Shot In An Automobile
    Bankers Control Several Major Auto Firms
    The "Quad" Truck Has Many New Innovations
    A DuPont Executive Buys Some General Motors Stock
    Good Roads Project Hits A Snag

1915 112
    Budd And Dodge Form A Unique Arrangement
    Cadillac Modernizes With A V-8
    Packard, Cadillac And Dodge Are The Icing On The Cake
    Durant Uses Chevrolet Motor Co. To Take Back General Motors
    Maxwell Sponsors Eddie Rickenbacker
    Charles T. Jeffery Survives The Lusitania Sinking
    The Most Famous Ad Appears
    Studebaker Designs Its Second Car

1916 122
    Nash Bows Out Of General Motors As Durant Resumes Control
    Henry Ford Antagonizes The Dodge's Into Filing Suit
    Pancho Villa Is Used To Test Mechanized Warfare
    Wilson's Re-Election Invites U.S. Into Europe's War

1917 126
    Brass Radiators No Longer Seen On New Fords
    DuPont Invests Heavily In General Motors Stock
    Durant Underestimates Henry Leland's Patriotism
    World War I Is The Cover For Financial Investors In Russia

1918 132
    Walter Marr And C. H. Wills Leave Their Respective Jobs
    Maxwell And Chalmers Make A Five Year Agreement
    Francis E. Stanley Succumbs To Auto Accident Injuries
    Henry Ford Runs For The U.S. Senate
    Many Car Makers Use V-8 And V-12 Engines For A While
    Durant's Power Is At Its Peak
1919 149
    Durant Underestimates Walter Chrysler's Sincerity
    Oregon Invents Gasoline Tax
    Henry Ford Tries, But Fails To Trick His Stockholers
    The Leland Father And Son Team Decides To Build Another Car
    One Of The Factors Contributing To "Roaring '20's" Spending
    The "Essex" Crackerbox Sedan, By Hudson, Starts A Trend
1920 153
    Both The Dodge Brothers Are Taken By Death
    The Willys' Challenge Lures Chrysler From "Retirement"
    Durant Is Ousted From G.M. The Final Time
    Gaston Chevrolet, Louis' Brother, Gets A Short Lived Honor
    Studebaker Ceases Production Of Its Horse-drawn Vehicles
    Henry Ford Causes His Own Dealers Much Anxiety
1921 156
    The Dodge Brothers Company Continues Without Its Founders
    Woodrow Wilson Buys A Used Car
    Durant Starts Another Auto Company
    Chrysler Goes From Willys To Maxwell-Chalmers
    The Lincoln Motor Co. Is Unjustly Taxed Into Receivership
1922
    Henry Ford Gets Rid Of Henry Leland
    Chrysler Gets The Maxwell Flaws Corrected
    Durant Motors Names A Car In Honor Of Flint, Michigan
    One Of Charles Kettering's Few Mistakes
1923 163
    Mr. Chrysler Finalizes Details To Bring Out The "Chrysler" Car
    Packard Starts A Trend With Their Straight Eight Engine
    What The Term "Assembled Car" Means
    Durant's Car Companies Pass Their Peak In Popularity
    Henry Ford's Power Is At Its Peak
    Cadillac Establishes The Flat Rate Labor System
1924 173
    Buick Imitates, But "Only Packard Can Build A Packard"
    The Quiet Stanley Scoops The Others With "Juice" Brakes
    Kettering Shows His Genius In Selling DUCO
1925 180
    Australian Brothers Use G.M. Cars Across The Syrian Desert
    Henry Ford's Refusal To Change Lets Chevrolet Get Ahead
    The Dodge Brothers' Estates Sell To Bankers

The Late 1920's 192
    Original Pioneers Mostly Gone
    A Future President Endorses An Automobile
    Mechanical Improvements In The 1920's
    Balloon Tires
    Four Wheel Brakes
    Hyrdraulic Brakes
    Enclosed Brakes
    Standardizing The Gearshift
    No Clash Shifting
    Windshield Wipers
    Stop Lights
    Hydraulic Shock Absorbers
    The Mechanical Fuel Pump

The Demise Of The Independent Auto Manufacturers 209
    Potential Auto Market Still Not Saturated
    Politics Gets Into Highway Design And Routes
    Better Roads Role In Improving Future Car Designs
    Why "Franklin" and "Willys-Knight" Failed
    The Air-Cooled Franklin, A Failure
    Sleeve Valves In The Knight Engine, A Failure
    The Oakland V-8 Becomes The Pontiac V-8

The 1930's 227
    Cars Become More Comfortable And Dependable
    The Weird Looking Airflow
    Lincoln-Zephyr Copies Airflow Body Idea
    The Cadillac Sixteen
    Nash Motors Survives The Depression
    Inventor's Names Given To Famous Products
    Men Using Names And Initials On Their Products
    The Model "A" Ford And The Ten Dollar Bill
    History Now Ended

Purpose

The purpose of this book is to inform as well as to entertain. It is meant to be a history of the early days of the men and the companies in the automobile industry in the United States whose names are still household words.

It does not contain statistics such as wheel bases, engine displacements, bore and stroke sizes, horsepower and the like. It is meant for the red-blooded person interested in this aspect of the culture and history of the United States. It is meant to appeal to everyone, not necessarily the automobile enthusiast.

How Detroit Changed History concerns cars built in the United States only. While at one time, MERCEDES, and later ROLLS-ROYCE, and today VOLKSWAGEN and others were assembled in this country, for use primarily in this country, and although some supplies for these U.S. assembled cars were purchased in this country, MERCEDES-BENZ, ROLLS-ROYCE, and VOLKWAGEN are still foreign cars and therefore not covered in this book.

Many of the stories are old chestnuts and familiar to many people as part of history. Many, many more stories are little known and part of the men's personal lives. Many of the early pioneers in the auto industry knew each other and worked for each other at one time or another. A definite effort has been made to show how the different things that happened to all of these pioneers all fit together and are intertwined.

The Mercedes was assembled in this country for a short time; this was about 15 years before the merger with Benz. In the 1920's Rolls-Royce was also assembled in this country. The German Volkswagen, the French Renault, and the Japanese Honda are presently being assembled in the United States. Other Japanese firms are considering the idea.

Introduction

To fully appreciate the men and the times mentioned in this book, we must look at a bit of United States History. When the "New World" was discovered, it was something never dreamed of.

The quickest and best means of transportation for centuries was the horse, whether ridden or used to pull something else on wheels. But the horse could only go so far and so fast. Then came the steam engine and the railroad locomotive. This played a tremendous part in the development of our culture in this country as it enabled people, entire families, to visit each other. Salesmen were able to vastly expand their horizons and bring the latest products and inventions to the frontier. During the "War Between the States" the railroads showed how valuable mass transportation really was and that it could be so much faster than the horse.

The largest people mover was the train which moved only from town to town. The invention of the bicycle allowed people to be independent of train schedules, coming and going around town and to the next town whenever they pleased, not subject to crowds and timetables. This started the bicycle craze or fad in this country in the late 1870's, which ran its course, becoming more and more frantic until it reached its peak in the 1890's, then tapered down soon after 1900. Railroads were still necessary and important for moving large groups of people and goods or merchandise for distances over 25 miles at reasonable speeds.

The "invention" of the automobile fascinated most men and in their eagerness to own one, how poorly made or how poorly suited it was to their particular needs did not seem to matter as they all wanted to try their hand at tinkering. As simple as automobiles were then, compared to today's automobiles, they were the most complex piece of machinery most people had ever seen, let alone being able to buy for themselves. While there were vacuum sweepers, and washing machines, and even phonographs, an automobile was made up of several different and complicated units that had to work together and do so in unison in order for the automobile to go.

Since it took men with money to get an automobile company started, the trend was to build cars to sell at fairly high prices in order to get a return on their investment. The reasoning was also that only wealthy people could afford automobiles and were already used to the best. Only a few realized that it would be the ordinary, hard working family man who would save his money to buy a car thereby establishing the volume of sales to make enough profit for a company to stay in business. Some companies never did learn this and consequently went broke; although the cars they sold were very well built, but were also very expensive. Others made an attempt in the mid 1930's but eventually went back to high-priced cars only and then went under.

Since most of the early pioneers in the auto industry were mechanics or tinkerers to some extent, very few were wealthy and therefore had to do something to raise the necessary working capital. Some, such as the Stanley twins and also Mr. Buick, sold existing businesses they owned and used that money to get into the automobile manufacturing business. The Stanley's succeeded in doing this but Mr. Buick failed. Mr. Buick then did what many other of the early pioneers did, he took in men as partners who had money to invest.

Whether partners were businessmen or bankers, all the auto men learned that whosoever controls the money controls the company. Mr. Olds learned this and so did Mr. Buick. While their companies had their particular names on the front doors of their particular companies, each of them eventually had little to do with the direction the companies took.

Circa 1890 "BONE CRUSHER" Type Bicycle

There were no brakes; you had to pedal slower, then jump off when you wanted to stop. These bicycles did not appeal to ladies or sensible gentlemen. Bicycles became popular when both wheels were the same size and had brakes and pneumatic tires. The Dodge brothers made bicycles before they became associated with Mr. Olds or Mr. Ford. Mr. Pierce also made bicycles as well as other items containing strong wire before getting into the automobile business. Among the wire items made by Pierce were bird cages.

Source: *Smithsonian Institution*

Circa 1770 Cugnot Artillery Tractor

What historians generally agree to be the first "self-propelled" vehicle that was anywhere near practical was this French Army artillery tractor. Since it was not designed to carry passengers, it cannot be considered an automobile.

The "Y" shaped object, sticking straight up in front of the bench seat, is the steering control which required both hands. Over 130 years later, Henry Ford built a racing car with a similar type of steering control.

The invention of the differential, which enables wheels on the same axle to go around corners at different speeds, was still over 100 years in the future, which explains why all the driving mechanism was on one wheel. The invention of the steering-knuckle king pin, which enables two wheels to turn while the axle remains stationary, was still over 100 years in the future, and this explains why the vehicle only had one front wheel.

Both Mr. Olds and Mr. Buick left the firms with their names on them for exactly this reason. So did Mr. Louis Chevrolet who never really controlled the company but had his name on it and also on the car.

Some historians maintain that the gasoline engine had less to do with the advent of the automobile before the 1890's than did the evolvement of the bicycle. Their reasoning is that with the popularity of the bicycle came the availability of a mechianical thing which was designed solely for the purpose of individuals being able to transport themselves mechanically from one place to another. Almost anyone could afford a bicycle, whether new or second hand.

Large groups of cyclists, who looked upon bicycling as a sport, formed groups to campaign for better roads. They also strived for roads to be marked, and for reliable maps to be made available. Those efforts resulted in more enjoyable cycling for families as well as for the sportsmen. Bicycle manufacturers became highly competitive. Naturally, those companies which gave the most value for the money succeeded. Installing brakes on bicycles made them much more acceptable, especially to ladies.

In addition to the development of mechanical features of bicycles came developments in tires. The poor roads caused much tire trouble. The primitive tire manufacturing procedures available in the 1890's left much to be desired.

The effect of the bicycle business on the automobile business was mainly to call attention to the need for improved roads and tires. While the surface had only been scratched by the cyclists, the development trends had been set. While it took over fifteen years for the gasoline engine to be developed enough and altered enough to be used to power a land vehicle, several bicycle manufacturers made the transition to automobile manufacturing. The two Dodge brothers, whose name is still being placed on new cars today, is one example. Another is "Rambler" which is the same company from which the present American Motors Corporation traces its heritage.

I have heard the question many times "Who invented the automobile?". The correct answer is that no one individual is responsible. It must first be determined what is meant by the word "automobile". A French Army Captain built what today would be called an artillery tractor back in 1769. It was steam-driven and went about two miles an hour. It was pulling a cannon when it went out of control and hit a wall. Two years later, in 1771, Captain Cugnot either rebuilt that one or built a second one which also met with an accident. The project was then abandoned. This was a self-propelled vehicle and is generally considered to be the first one that was even remotely practical. It cannot be considered an "automobile" since it was not meant to carry passengers.

In England, by the late 1820's, many omnibusses were going from one city to another hauling a dozen or so passengers each. They were also steam-driven. The knowledge of making precision machine tools to make good parts with close tolerances was still a few years in the future, and so was the development of steel alloys needed for the various steam generating and steam engine parts. Small parts, such as for rifles and pistols, could be made exact and interchangeable and Colt, Smith & Wesson, and Eli Whitney were all doing this in the United States. Eli Whitney made muskets for the Continental Army before he invented the cotton gin. One of the reasons Whitney was awarded the contract for muskets was that he made them with interchangeable parts. Large machines like the English omnibusses, for example, were mostly individually fitted. When a new part was needed, it was individually made and spare parts were all but unknown.

The invention of the gasoline engine came in the late 1870's. 1876 was a presidential election year and one of the most scandal-plagued administrations this country had seen until that time, that of Ulysses S. Grant, would be voted out to make room for Rutherford B. Hayes.

Two of the inventions which were entered in the Philadelphia Centennial Expositon of 1876 were destined to have great impact. Both were somewhat crude by today's standards and both needed help from people other than their original inventors to get them practical and salable.

One of these inventions was the telephone of Mr. Watson and Mr. Bell which took Mr. Edison to make practical. The other invention was the two-cycle gasoline engine of Mr. George Brayton. It attracted the attention of patent attorney George B. Selden who conceived the idea of using it to power a road vehicle. Three years later, in 1879, he applied for a patent on a complete vehicle using an engine which ran on liquid fuel plus having a clutch to disengage the engine so it could run while the vehicle was standing still. There was also a steering mechanism for the vehicle.

Further development of a self-propelled vehicle took place in Europe for two main reasons. First, there was a better highway system throughout Europe whereas the biggest concentration of people in the United States was in the northeast and what few good roads did exist were mostly in that area. The second reason was that while Mr. Bayton's *two-cycle* engine had appeared in the United States two years ealier, it was not as practical for propelling a road vehicle as was the *four-cycle* engine of Mr. Otto, a German. To be more exact, Mr. Otto's engine was a four-cycle internal combustion engine. Its inventor was Mr. Nicholas Otto, in Germany, in 1878. Furthermore, at that time gasoline was a waste by-product of the petroleum industry and was dumped because it was too explosive to handle safely. Benzol and gasoline were sometimes mixed together as a fuel for the Otto engine. Naturally, the first engines were very crude and the idea of using them to propel a road vehicle did not come right away. A spin off of Mr. Otto's engine was the diesel.

It would be virtually impossible to list all those who had built a self-propelled vehicle in this country, as quite a few were just one of a kind made by backyard tinkerers. Since these tinkerers did not have the desire or could not see the possibilities of manufacturing them commercially, or could not raise the money, they did not pursue the endeavor beyond the first one or two vehicles.

Those whose names are more likely to be remembered now were Ransom E. Olds, Henry Ford, Alexander Winton, the Stanley twins, Elwood Haynes with the Apperson brothers. All built at least one car by the mid 1890's in this country. While only one was anything other than a gasoline-powered car, they were probably attracting more attention because of their noise making and being more of a novelty. Steam power was by far the best known since railroads had been using steam engines for many years. There had been no effort to reduce the weight of a steam railroad locomotive, as the more weight the more traction on the comparatively thin driving wheels of the locomotives. Dead weight was needed to hold them down and aided in traction when starting from a dead stop. The basic steam principle had to be reduced considerably in weight and size to work in an automobile.

By the mid 1890's electric vehicle development was also under way. Now, ninety years later, electric vehicles are still not in widespread use for the same reason that they never caught on before. They had a very limited range before they ran out of "juice" and must be re-charged. Also, their batteries were very expensive and very heavy. A group of promoters made electrically powered Hansom Cabs for use in large cities, primarily in the East — New York, Boston, Philadelphia. In some, the driver sat above and out in the open behind the passenger compartment which was enclosed. Some had electric motors driving the front wheels and were steered by the rear wheels; others had just the opposite arrangement. They made it a policy to change batteries after every trip, taking them out for charging and installing a freshly charged set. This went a long way to show how impractical the electric vehicles were; but by the mid 1890's, they were better than anything else available.

G. B. SELDEN.
ROAD ENGINE.

No. 549,160.

Patented Nov. 5, 1895.

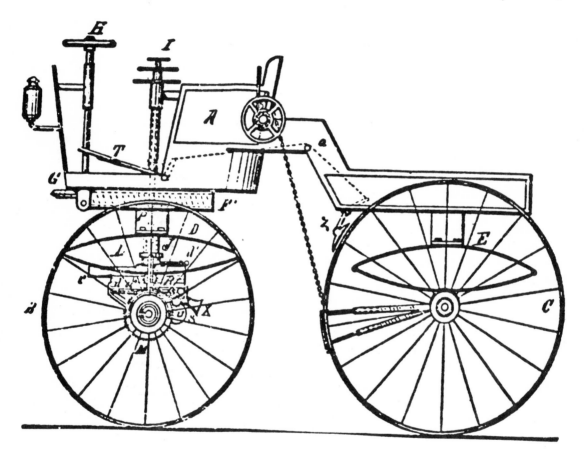

1894 HAYNES

A confident Elwood Haynes of Kokomo in the car he first drove on July 4, 1894.

It has never been determined who made the first automobile in the United States. During the 1930's a lot of study and research was done and it was narrowed down considerably. Some say Haynes-Apperson, some say the Duryea's, and some say others did. Haynes and Apperson disagreed in their later years as to who was the most important, each saying that the other was just there.

Mr. Elwood G. Haynes of Kokomo, Indiana, wanted a faster way of getting around than a horse would take him. He was a chemist and a metallurgist engineer and drew up plans for a self-propelled buggy. He bought a one cylinder, two cycle engine and a buggy, and got the Apperson brothers to follow his plans and put the vehicle together. The two brothers had to show Haynes that certain things would not work exactly as he had planned, so the design was modified as they went along. By July 4, 1894, the completed vehicle was ready for a road test. They hitched it to a horse and towed it several miles out of town to a rather desolate spot on the road, then started it and made a triumphant drive back into Kokomo on Pumpkinville Pike.

There is no Pumpkinville on modern road maps of Indiana, but since a lot of small towns in that area end in "ville", it is quite possible that there was a town by that name in 1894. One of the Apperson brothers' employees who helped build this car was Jonathan D. Maxwell, who later played an important role in the early auto industry.

In 1887 Mr. Olds tested his first cars in secrecy. He chose before dawn darkness to avoid embarrassment if they broke down.

Each of the two Duryea brothers claimed to be the most important one in the building of their first car. This difference separated them in their later years and, as far as I have been able to tell, neither ever backed down. They refused to associate with each other, and each went to his grave with this bitterness toward his brother.

Actually, people all over the world were experimenting with Mr. Otto's and Mr. Brayton's inventions and several in different areas, who had never heard of each other, were discovering almost exactly the same things at almost exactly the same time. While some were trying to improve the gasoline engine, others were improving the steam engine, and still others, the electric motor.

Except for Mr. Olds and a few others whose names are no longer household words, the evolvement or development of a car or automobile as such (not an artillery tractor or omnibus) began in the period of the early 1890's.

Messrs, Duryea, Durant, Packard, Nash, Olds, Ford, and Dodge were all born between 1860 and 1870. Messrs Willys, Chrysler, Kettering, Winton, and Chevrolet were all born between 1870 and 1880.

There was enough interest in the "automobile" by 1895 for the Chicago Times-Herald newspaper to put on their publicity stunt race on Thanksgiving Day, but it was snowed under. It was actually more of an endurance contest. Whether there had been snow or not, an endurance contest is all that it would have been. Since there were no types or classes of the different sizes or weights of the cars entered, it was every one for himself. Because of the heavy snow, it was not as much of a proving ground as had been desired, but it was significant enough to attract considerable attention at the time. Several of the entrants did not participate as their vehicles could not negotiate the slippery streets. Eleven were entered, six actually started the race, and two finished — the fastest averaging under seven miles an hour for the less than fifty miles.

Many different kinds of motive power have been tried, the more common ones being gasoline, steam, and electric power. There were also different mechanically-driven vehicles, which seemed pretty "far out," bordering on schemes for perpetual motion machines. No one knew at the time which type of power was going to be practical or catch the public's fancy.

1895 DURYEA

Charles E. Duryea shown in the car in which he won the Thanksgiving Day race in Chicago in 1895. This automobile bears only a slight resemblance to the first vehicle built by the Duryea brothers during 1893-94.

Each had its own merits and each had its own drawbacks; therefore each had to be tested. The backers of the mechanical freaks found out fairly soon that these machines were just that. Those who developed one particular part of a car which excelled sometimes had to find out through expensive experience that it took more than one superior part of a car to make the whole car good. The most common mistake was (and still is) concentrating on the engine. While no one can deny the importance of a good engine, it is of little value if the steering does not work right, or the transmission, or the rear axle, or the brakes give trouble. All units have to be made to work together in harmony. This was achieved only by trial and error and experience.

The Mid 1890's

The Beginning Of A New Industry

Let's take a look at what our future automobile executives were doing in 1895: The two Dodge brothers were in their mid and upper twenties and worked in their father's Detroit machine shop. Ransom E. Olds had bought out his father's interest in their Lansing machine shop which had been making stationary engines; he was thirty. Henry M. Leland, just over fifty, was the senior partner in the Detroit machine shop of Leland and Faulkner that made gasoline engines, both stationary and marine. Louis Chevrolet, who would be seventeen on Christmas Day, was just getting involved in bicycle racing in France. George N. Pierce was in the business of making things out of strong wire, first bird cages, then wheels for bicycles, and then the entire bicycle. Walter P. Chrysler, twenty, was an apprentice (steam) railroad mechanic in Kansas. William C. Durant, 34, was the senior partner of the Durant-Dort Carriage Co., the largest business in Flint, Michigan, and primarily responsible for Flint's being known as the "Vehicle City" as Durant-Dort made over half the 100,000 horse-drawn vehicles in Flint. Charles W. Nash, 31, was working as a foreman in the Durant-Dort Carriage Co. in Flint. Charles F. Kettering, 19, was just finishing at Ohio State University with degrees in mechanical and electrical engineering. David D. Buick, 41, was tinkering, as usual, in his plumbing supply firm in Detroit while dreaming of the automobile. Henry Ford, 31, was spending his spare time and money on building his first vehicle, and working as a self-taught engineer for the Detroit Electric Company. James W. Packard, 32, was making electrical parts in Warren, Ohio. Frances E. and Freelan O. Stanley, twins, age 46, were making dry plates for their photo supply business in New England and looking over every automobile they could. Thomas B. Jeffery was designing a car in the Rambler Bicycle Co. which he owned, in Chicago.

It is necessary to mention a few names that are no longer household words because of the effect they had on those whose names were still going to be familiar almost 100 years later. In particular, Nash, Packard, Pierce, Winton, Jeffery, Studebaker, Maxwell, and others all played an important role in the development of the automobile in the United States, and all had cars named for them. All the companies using those names have been out of business at least twenty years, so the current generation of students in school did not know them when they were producing new cars. Some companies went out of business around the time of their namesake's retirement while others left an organization behind which was able to carry on several more years. A few other men had a definite influence on the automobile business and were actively engaged in it but never had a car named for them. Some of them were Henry M. Leland, Charles F. Kettering, Roy D. Chapin, and William C. Durant. Henry M. Leland was the main driving force behind the start of the two most famous prestigous cars that this country has ever known, Cadillac and Lincoln. Charles F. Kettering was a genius if there ever was one, and a brilliant inventor. He was to the automobile business what Thomas Edison was to electricity. The city of Kettering, Ohio, just south of Dayton, was named for him. Roy D. Chapin was one of the original partners and the driving force behind the Hudson Motor Car Co. The Hudson, and its cheaper model, the Essex, had a great influence on changing the automobile business in the 1920's.

William C. Durant was the only one of the names mentioned above to have a car named for him. By the 1920's Durant had lost interest in the automobile business. It may seem a contradiction to say that he waited until he lost interest in the automobile business before having a car with his name on it, but that is exactly what happened. By that time, he was more interested in manipulating the stock market and merely wanted to keep his name before the public. The public had associated him with the automobile business since the early days of the industry, so the easiest way for him to keep the public confidence was with an automobile company with his name. In the end it played a large part in his personal downfall.

The Ideal Car Size

The idea of what size car to build didn't occur to anyone until after the turn of the century. While it is true that there were gasoline and steam and electricity as motive power, no one was sure which would work best. The main efforts were concentrated on getting the machinery to be reasonably dependable, or at least as dependable as the competition. The larger gasoline and electric and steam power plants for automobiles were developed around 1904. The roads in this country were so poor, outside the cities, that the extra power developed by the new larger engines could not be used for much more than to move the additional weight of heavier and fancier limousines, which were primarily limited to the large cities. Mr. George N. Pierce, whose company later built one of the largest automobile engines this country has ever seen, started out building the one cylinder Pierce "Motorette" which was a small buggy-size car. The first Cadillacs were small, so were the first cars built by Mr. Packard, Mr. Ford, and Mr. Olds.

The United States was primarily an agricultural or farming country, therefore it had to develop its own type of car. In Europe, where good roads had existed for hundreds of years, the limousine was reasonably well-suited for those few who could afford them. The Industrial Revolution really got under way in this country in the mid 1870's with the perfection of machine tools and the inventive genius of Thomas Edison, George Westinghouse, and others. The United States did not reach its full potential and surpass Europe in technology until between 1910 and 1915. Europe's involvement in World War I was only part of the reason the United States passed them. The big reasons were that the United States needed to develop and build its own car for its own use and that there were available the contributions of great inventors like Edison and Westinghouse who had eager and ready markets for any mechanical things that would make life easier, especially farm life.

It did not occur to Europeans to make precision parts, one exactly like the next one, on a large scale. Instead, they employed fitters who could file down the part by hand until it fit the part next to it the way it should. The wage standards were lower, so it was not a financial burden on the manufacturer to have fitters instead of expensive machine tools and skilled men to use them. It was a burden on the car owner, however, when he had to buy a replacement part, because if it wouldn't fit he would have to get a mechanic to file it to fit the way it was supposed to. In the United States, meantime, precision machinery meant that one skilled machinist, using high quality raw materials and proper machine tools, could turn out quite a few parts exactly alike with no need for fitters to put everything together.

From 1895 to 1905, many things had a direct bearing on the formation of the auto industry. The trends were set by the events of history. Of course there were a few exceptions. Generally, however, the auto industry became big business, but only those would survive with high production facilities and the foresight to expand and keep increasing production as the demand increased. Only the wealthy men, who obtained their wealth from other sources, had the foresight to back the auto producers of the era. Bankers took a very skeptical and conservative view of investing in the auto business although many of these same bankers owned cars themselves. It wasn't until after 1905, generally, that bankers realized that maybe money could be made from automobile manufacturing.

Doctors, on the other hand, took the opposite view. They needed a faster way of getting around than the horse and buggy provided, as in those days doctors still made house calls. The first Buick was bought by a physician in Flint in the summer of 1904. The first two cars sold by the Ford Motor Co. (advertised as Fordmobiles) were bought by doctors in the summer of 1903, one by a dentist in Chicago, and the other by a physician in Akron.

During the period between 1895 and 1905, companies already engaged in some form of manufacturing branched out into either building their own cars or going into partnership with others who had designed cars and needed manufacturing facilities. Some of the companies which had already specialized in making certain types of parts used in car manufacture expanded even further into complete car manufacture. Studebaker is one example of such a company partnership which will be discussed further in a later chapter.

Let's return to the mid 1890's when polka dots were all the style in both women's dresses and shirt waists.

1896

Bicycles Greatly Improved

Two competitive bicycle manufacturers, Columbia and Pierce, each approached the Leland and Faulkner Machine Shop in Detroit for help in making silent gears for their bicycles and each received a superior part for his particular need. All three companies would play an important role in the infant auto industry in just a very few years.

King, Then Ford Each Drive Cars In Detroit

The first week of March, Charles B. King drove his "car" in Detroit. Less than three months later Henry Ford drove his first car in Detroit.

Mr. Ford's landlord happened by just as Henry's vehicle was ready for its first test drive. One problem was that the building where Henry had put it all together did not have a big enough door to get the completed vehicle through. He was somewhat like the fellow who built a boat in his basement. Henry started to chop down a brick wall to get the vehicle out. The landlord started to object, but Henry convinced him of the importance of the project, and legend has it that the landlord helped tear down his own wall and even helped Henry push to get the car started.

Famous Bicycle Maker Begins Auto Manufacture

Colonel Albert Augustus Pope, who was already very wealthy from building the "Columbia" bicycle, started making electric cars and still used the name "Columbia."

1896 Quadracycle with Henry Ford

Henry Ford and his first automobile. This poto was taken before he sold the car. It is one of the few pictures showing Henry Ford smiling.

GENTLEMEM OUR COUNTRY

HENRY FORD AND HIS FIRST CAR.

1896 Quadracycle with Henry Ford

Although this is Henry Ford sitting in his first car, this photo was taken in 1905. Other photos of Henry taken around 1896 show him with a stylish handlebar moustache. Photos taken since shortly after the turn of the century show him without it. After he built this vehicle and knew he could make a better one, he sold this one. Later, after the Ford Motor Co. became a success, he traced its ownership and bought it back. It was during this second, permanent ownership that this photo was taken.

During Henry's lifetime this Quadracycle was rolled out to be photographed with various celebrities and with various milestone cars. This vehicle now resides in its place of honor in the Ford Museum in Dearborn.

"KING"
Gasoline Engines

No Oil Cups. Exhausts
Under Water. Noiseless.

COMPLETE LAUNCHES, YACHTS,
and WORKING BOATS.

THE CHARLES B. KING CO., Detroit, Mich.

Charles B. King was the first person to drive an "automobile" in the city of Detroit. It is said that he helped Henry Ford who drove his vehicle three months later, both in 1896.

A few years later King was employed by the Olds Motor Works for a time. King and a fellow Olds' engineer, Jonathan D. Maxwell were very instrumental in making the short-lived "Northern" automobile.

Source: *Smithsonian Institution*

1897 Olds

The driver's left hand is on the steering tiller while his right hand is on the handle which regulates the engine speed. Four vehicles like this were built by the Olds in 1897.

Charles Ainsley Becomes Detroit's First Used Car Buyer

Henry Ford sold his first vehicle to Charles Ainsley in Detroit for $200.00. Mr. Ainsley eventually sold it and several years later Henry Ford traced its ownership and bought it back. Henry Ford called his first vehicle a quadricycle.

The Stanley's Get Serious

The Stanley twins, Freelan and Francis, started designing their first car, that would be steam-powered.

1897

Mr. Packard Doesn't Like His New Winton Car

Alexander Winton, in Cleveland, was having trouble with the reliability of the cars he had built. Two customers had complained. One was James W. Packard who had bought Winton number 12. Mr. Packard's dissatisfaction with the Winton led him to build a car of his own. To prove his cars were reliable, Mr. Winton drove one of them 800 miles from Cleveland to New York City. The trip took ten days. Mr. Winton became famous for his drive. He built a few racing cars with which he later competed with Henry Ford. This helped get Ford's name before the public and keep Winton's there.

Studebaker Looks Into The Automobile Idea

On May 12, Studebaker's Board of Directors authorized experimenting with automobiles with the possibility of building them.

The Olds Motor Works Comes Into Existence

August 4 saw the Olds Motor Works founded in Lansing with Ransom E. Olds' name but with very little of his money invested in it.

Rambler Experimental Car Is Completed

Thomas B. Jeffery, who had built the "Rambler" bicycle in Chicago, built his first experimental car.

The Luxury of Locomotion

is embodied in

THE WINTON
MotorCarriage

They are handsome, easy riding, durable, highly economical and under perfect control.

14 of them are in actual use and giving splendid satisfaction.

Variable Speed Hydro-Carbon Motor.

Price $1,000.   *No Agents.*

Place your order to secure prompt delivery.

☞ *Write for Catalogue.*

THE WINTON MOTOR CARRIAGE CO., Cleveland, Ohio.

Of the 14 Winton Motor Carriages "in actual use," one was not giving the "splendid satisfaction" claimed in this 1898 ad. Mr. James W. Packard had bought Winton #12. He built his own car correcting what he considered the shortcomings of his Winton. He founded the Packard Motor Car Co. in 1899.

1898

The Stanley's Sell Out To Eastman Kodak

The Stanley Motor Carriage Company went into business making light steam carriages in West Newton, Mass., near Boston. The Stanley brothers, identical twins, had sold their photo supply business and patents to Eastman Kodak and used that money to go into the automobile business.

1899

The Stanley's Get An Offer They Can't Resist

The Stanley twins sold their automobile business to two partners for a quarter of a million dollars and agreed to stay on and run the place and not to manufacturer steam cars for two years on their own. The new company took the name Locomobile.

The President Goes For A Silent Ride

President William McKinley rode in a Locomobile steamer, becoming the first United States President to ride in an automobile while in office.

In 1899, William McKinley became the first president of the United States to ride in an automobile. It was in a car identical to the Locomobile Steamer shown in this illustration. The car had been designed by the Stanley twins and was a carbon copy of their Stanley Steamer.

The Stanley's sold their company to the gentlemen listed in this ad, went to work for them, and promised not to make their own car again for two years. Later the Stanley's bought the company back and started making their Stanley Steamers again. Locomobile switched to gasoline power.

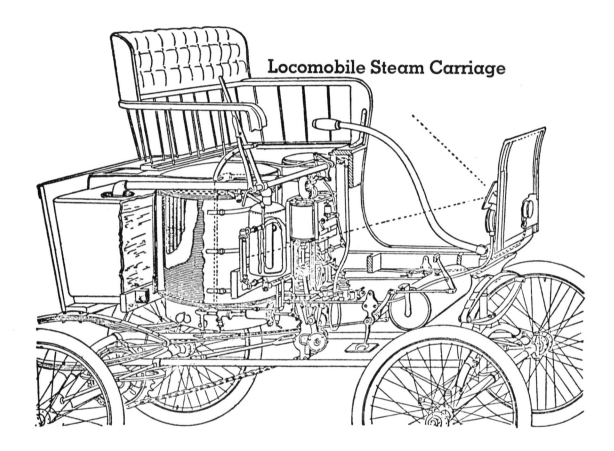

Locomobile Steam Carriage

Locomobile Carriage

Cutaway drawing shows the Stanley designed Locomobile carriage. It was almost identical to the Stanley. The very early Stanley's and Locomobile's had the engine mounted vertically under the seat and drove the rear axle through a single chain. A couple of years later, Stanley mounted the engine horizontally under the rear floor attached directly to the rear axle.

1900

Locomobile Switches To Gasoline Power

After only a very short time building steam powered automobiles, Locomobile decided to switch to gasoline power.

Mr. Packard Builds His First Car

James W. Packard built his first car in Warren, Ohio and the company became known as the Ohio Automobile Co. Packard retained his Packard Electric Co.

Auto Show Held In New York City

The first automobile show to be held in New York City opened at the old Madison Square Garden on November 3.

Popular President Re-Elected

One of the most popular presidents this country has ever known, William McKinley, was re-elected on November 6.

1901

Oil Discovered In Texas

On January 10, oil was discovered in Spindletop, near Beaumont, Texas.

Olds Fire A Blessing In Disguise

On March 9, fire destroyed the new Olds factory. It was the worst fire the City of Detroit had ever seen until that time. An alert young time-keeper, with the good Irish names of James J. Brady, saw an experimental model parked near a door and pushed it outside. It was the *only* car saved! Some plans and blueprints, etc. escaped the fire because they were in a vault. Since the summer was the only time to use a car in those days and since the summer selling season was fast approaching, Olds had to act quickly. He ordered engines and transmissions from the Leland and Faulkner Machine Shop in Detroit, also from the Dodge Brothers Machine Shop in Detroit. Olds ordered other parts from other suppliers and was able to stay in business. The one experimental model was now their *only* model; it became known as the Merry Oldsmobile.

David Buick's Life Starts Downhill

Although it may seem strange to say it now, Mr. David D. Buick made his greatest contribution to the world *before* he ever thought of getting into the automobile business. He had always been interested in mechanical things and had a few inventions and patents to his credit. By the time he was about 30, he and a fellow named William Sherwood found themselves owners of a plumbing supply business in Detroit. Mr. Buick designed some of the fixtures himself. Bear in mind that what plumbing did exist in the 1880's was out of doors. The bath tub being brought inside and used on Saturday night, as we have seen depicted in movies and T.V., is probably pretty close to the way it was. The tub was probably a low grade of steel and had to be carefully cleaned before every use as it developed rust very quickly. The personal washing one did was to pour water into a china bowl especially made for that purpose and wash every day with soap and a wash cloth, followed up by the Saturday night bath.

In the early 1890's Buick unlocked the secret of applying procelain to cast iron and steel. This led the way for bathroom and kitchen fixtures to have this coating on them which could be kept clean and therefore sanitary and allowed the fixtures to be brought inside the house. This was one of the most important single inventions of the previous one hundred years, if not all time, ranking equally with the wheel, gunpowder, the printing press, the piano, the X-ray, the telephone, the cathode ray (radio) tube, the talking machine, the electric light, the transistor, etc., for it actually changed the way the world lived.

Buick eventually became sole owner of the business. By the turn of the century he heard about recent developments of the gasoline engine and how it was being installed in different horseless carriages of the time. His experimental and inventive nature took over and he lost interest in his plumbing supply business. In quick succession by April, 1901, he had sold the plumbing supply company and had formed the Buick Auto Vim and Power Company of Detroit. By the end of 1901 he had built one or two cars with a two-cylinder engine with the help of a brilliant engineer, Walter Marr.

Henry Ford Goes Into Business For The Second Time

The Detroit Automobile Company, with Henry Ford as chief engineer, had begun in 1899 but floundered in late 1900 because the financial backers wanted cars to be sold and some profit on their investment. Instead, there had been only experimenting and a race car or two. New financial backers were located and the Henry Ford Company began in late 1901.

Roy Chapin Shows That Olds Has Recovered From Its Fire

A young college graduate whose hobby was photography began working at the Olds factory filing down transmission gears so the teeth would mesh. He made the publicity pictures for the Olds Motor Works in addition to his other duties. The first week of November, the automobile show was scheduled for New York City. Mr. Olds thought it would be a good publicity stunt to have a car driven from Detroit to New York City. Alexander Winton had

Illus 35-36

1901 Winton Racer

This was a racer built by Alexander Winton, who was one of the best known people in the auto industry in 1901. He had been building cars to sell, not racers, since 1898. Winton raced this car against one made by Henry Ford in 1901, and Ford won.

The face and fingers of the fellow on the car's left belong to the mechanic, who was half kneeling and half crouching on a platform or running board. The riding mechanic served two needs. One was to repair the car if it broke down during the race. The other was to add stability or ballast to the car as it rounded the flat, oval-shaped dirt track. The mechanic's added weight counteracted centrifical force somewhat to keep the car from skidding or upsetting as it went around the curves at high speed.

recently made a name for himself by driving a Winton from Cleveland to New York City and Detroit was further away from New York than Cleveland. Olds chose the young photographer to make the run. He was Roy Chapin who later became head of the Hudson Motor Car Co. Young Roy Chapin made the trip; it took a week. When he arrived at the Olds headquarters in New York's Waldorf Astoria, the doorman refused to let him in because he was so mud-spattered and dirty. He went around to another entrance, found Mr. Olds and the party anxiously waiting for him. Everyone was jubilant that young Roy Chapin and the little Olds made it. It showed the world that Olds had fully recovered from the horrible fire earlier that spring. During the trip, every unit of the car needed some sort of repair or adjustment, yet young Roy Chapin was always able to fix it and keep going. The trip made such a profound impression on Roy Chapin that after he became president of Hudson, he devoted all of his spare time pioneering for good roads for the entire country.

The Stanley's Start Over Again

After Locomobile had switched to gasoline power, they had no more use for the former Stanley facilities. Locomobile had also opened another factory. So, in May, the Stanley's bought back all they had sold to Locomobile for a quarter million dollars for only $20,000.00; then they sold White some patents which they no longer needed for over half of their $20,000.00 investment. This put the Stanley's back into business for themselves, still making steam-powered cars.

1902

How The "Cadillac" Car Came Into Being

The Leland and Faulkner Machine Shop had been building the Olds parts exactly as ordered. After a while they found that they could make a few changes here and there and "hop up" the one-cylinder Olds engine from about four horsepower to about ten horsepower. Ten horsepower is not much by today's standards, but it was over a 100% increase at the time. Mr. Leland had his men put this more powerful engine in his own Oldsmobile and then he took it to the Oldsmobile plant and showed it to the executives there. They were very pleased with it until they learned how much more it would cost. Their reasoning was that they could not keep pace with orders now, so why make a more expensive car. This left Mr. Leland with a beautifully sweet-running engine and no place to put it to its proper use.

While Oldsmobile was buying parts from Mr. Leland's company and from the Dodge Brothers' company (both machine shops), Henry Ford's second attempt to enter the automobile business, the Henry Ford Company, was collapsing around him. Mr. Ford actually left the company in the spring of 1902, but the company itself went on a little after that.

In August of 1902, the former financial backers of Henry Ford decided to liquidate their assets and equipment and supplies and machinery, so they went to the one person they knew could tell them exactly what everything was worth, Mr. Henry Leland. The backers knew of his experience in building engines for many years, and that he was now building them for Oldsmobile. Mr. Leland agreed to make the appraisal for them. When he went to give them the appraisal, he also took along the engine he had "improved" from an Oldsmobile engine. He

1901 Riker Electric Ambulance

When President William McKinley was shot on September 6, 1901, while attending the Pan American Exposition, he was taken to the hospital in an electric ambulance, if not this one, one identical to it. It was McKinley's second ride in a motorized vehicle. He never rode in a gasoline-powered vehicle, yet both manufacturers later switched to gasoline power.

This vehicle was powered by two electric motors, one at each rear wheel; the right rear motor is clearly visible in this photo. The batteries were carried beneath the floor.

Just a few months after McKinley's assassination, Andrew L. Riker sold his company which had produced electric vehicles and went to work for Locomobile, that soon switched to gasoline-powered cars designed by Riker. A few years later, Locomobile decided to build high quality trucks. Not wanting to have the same name on their trucks as on their automobiles, as Packard and Pierce-Arrow had done, Locomobile named their truck "Riker."

Riker trucks were still rendering distinguished service during the military action of World War I.

convinced the backers that his engine was very dependable and more powerful than anything else its size and, that, with all the machinery and equipment they already had, coupled with his engine, plus a plant in which to build it, they should enter a new phase of the automobile business.

It just so happened that the city of Detroit was taken up with bicentennial fever in 1902 in much the same way that the entire country was more recently, in 1976. The reason was that the city of Detroit had been founded 201 years earlier, in 1701. They decided to name the new car after the Frenchman who had founded the city of Detroit, M. Cadillac. While this was going on, Henry Ford located still other financial backers and went back into the automobile business himself for the third, and what turned out to be his final time in late 1902. It is believed that maybe one experimental car of Ford's was running by the end of 1902 in Detroit; the chief designer was C. H. Wills.

The First "Rambler" Cars Appear

Mr. Thomas B. Jeffery had bought a former bicycle factory in Kenosha, Wisconsin, and began producing the "Rambler" car. Since Mr. Jeffery had made the Rambler bicycle in Chicago for about twenty years, he decided to stick with that successful name. He left the bicycle business at the same time he entered the automobile business.

The First "Studebaker" Cars Appear

After fifty years of making horse drawn vehicles, Studebaker made their first automobile; it was an electric. The great inventor Thomas A. Edison bought Studebaker number two.

Henry Ford Makes One Of His Wisest Employment Decisions

Sometime in late 1901 or early 1902, a young man answered a newspaper ad which Henry Ford had run for a draftsman. A restless young fellow named C. H. Wills was hired to fill the position. He was much more than a draftsman, having been educated in engineering and metallurgy as well as drafting. (Elwood Haynes who drove his car down Pumpkinville Pike into Kokomo on July 4, 1894, was also a metallurgist.) Mr. Ford could not afford to keep Mr. Wills on the payroll very long so he resigned, took another job, and worked for Henry Ford in the evening. Legend has it that poor Henry Ford could not even afford coal for the stove in the little shop where they worked, so the two of them would put on boxing gloves and spar with each other every hour or so for a few minutes to get the blood circulating back in their fingers. As we will see later, C. H. Wills was just as important to the early Ford Motor Company through the design and engineering section of the company as was James Couzens to the bookkeeping end of the company.

The Buick Company Is Floundering

There were two Briscoe brothers, Ben and Frank, who had a sheet metal business in Detroit. They made parts for several of the early auto makers of the area, such things as radiators, gas tanks, fenders, etc. The Briscoe brothers were intrigued by the infant industry but originally kept it as a sideline to their main item of manufacturing a new invention — the metal garbage can. In order to get them to put up money (after going through his own hundred

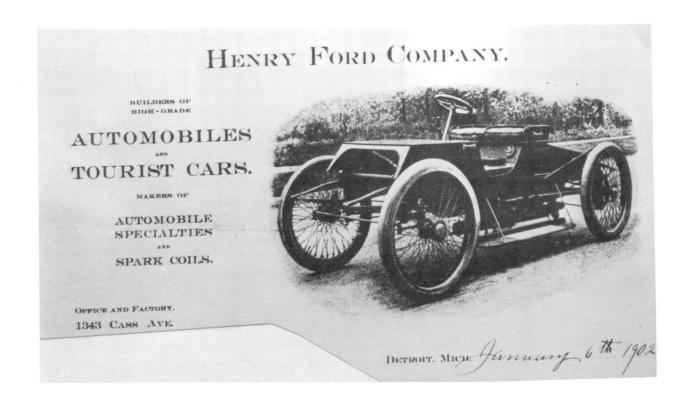

1902 Henry Ford Company

    This was the second of the three automobile companies started by Henry Ford. The picture and letterhead appear quite impressive, listing all that the company was able to produce. The term *touring car* had not yet become the common term, or else there was a misprint, as it is shown on the letterhead as *tourist car*. The car pictured here was one of the racers. With Henry Ford driving and Ed "Spider" Huff riding as mechanic in a part kneeling, part crouching position, using the handle shown here for his left hand. In 1901 they raced Alexander Winton and won; that victory helped to make Ford's name well known.

    Ford's financial backers wanted more cars built to sell than built to race. Henry's attitude was that race cars were needed to see which designs, etc. were dependable. Ford left the Henry Ford Company a few months later. It was from the remains of this that his former backers approached Henry M. Leland later in the year and the Cadillac Motor Co. was founded. The present Ford Motor Co. was established in the summer of 1903.

1903 Barney Oldfield and Henry Ford With Racer

Photo shows Henry Ford standing and Barney Oldfield seated in the racer, grasping the steering control handles. This was one of many Ford-built racers which helped make the Henry Ford name well known. Ford raced several of the cars himself during the early "turn of the century" years.

Barney Oldfield raced Ford's cars against Winton, and also raced Winton's cars. Oldfield's name became synonomous with speed. Among those who raced against him at various times were Louis Chevrolet and his brothers Gaston and Arthur Chevrolet.

1903 Winton Racer, Bullet # 2

This Winton racer was known as Bullet #2. Alexander Winton, himself, drove it in several races and won; Barney Oldfield also won several races with it.

The engine has eight cylinders. Two four-cylinder engines were bolted together end for end. The cylinders, easily visible in the photo, were mounted horizontally, instead of the more common practice of vertically.

thousand in about a year), David Buick promised the Briscoe's the first car made by the "new" Buick Manufacturing Company. It took almost a year to build it but it was finally ready in early 1903.

Two Automobile "Old Timers" Get Together

Two "old timers" in the automobile business got together and became partners in a new venture in the automobile business. These "old timers" were Charles B. King, who drove the first car in Detroit in 1896 a few months before Henry Ford, and the same Jonathan D. Maxwell who had helped the Haynes and Apperson men build their car in Kokomo in 1894. Both were now engineers at Oldsmobile (1902). Mr. Maxwell had designed the cooling system for the curved dash Mery Oldsmobile.

The car they made was called the Northern. There was also a third partner whose name, however, has never been a household word. The Northern had the same type of spring suspension with two springs running the length of the chassis as did the curved dash Merry Oldsmobile. It also had tiller steering and had no provision for a rear seat. It had a one-cylinder engine mounted in the center of the car, and the "Northern" had more than a slight resemblance to the Merry Oldsmobile.

1903

Cadillac, Buick, and Ford Make Modest Beginnings

Without the people involved in the automobile industry realizing it at the time, 1903 was going to be a turning point in the infant industry.

Cadillac began full production of their cars in the spring after having made three experimental cars. Cadillac's sales manager in 1903 was William Metzger, formerly with Oldsmobile, who would be the "M" in the E.M.F. car after having made a car with his own name on it.

The Ford Motor Company was not formally organized until June 16, 1903. Henry Ford put up no money, only a couple of race cars and the know-how he had plus a few patents. A major stock holder in the Ford Motor Co. at this time was a coal dealer, Alexander Malcomson, who had a hard-nosed bookkeeper named James Couzens, who also bought some Ford stock and was put in charge of Ford's books, partly to keep a frugal eye on Malcomson's money. One of the Ford Motor Company's most valuable employees came to be James Couzens. His hard-nosed common sense was the needed counter balance to the often strange acting Henry Ford, who was not accustomed to accounting procedures or handling large amounts of money.

The first advertising was in a magazine aimed at obtaining dealers and not read by the general public. The second series of ads was the first to appear before the general public and was approved by James Couzens, but not Henry Ford who, according to legend, objected to calling the car FORDMOBILE. He made it clear to Mr. Couzens that the name "Fordmobile" was never to be used again. It never was. Mr. Olds had the best known, most popular car in 1903, and simply added "mobile" behind his name to name the car. Mr. Ford's name also had

1903 Fordmobile

The first product of the Ford Motor Co. was advertisd once as "Fordmobile." The Oldsmobile was the best selling car in the country at the time; its name being derived by adding "mobile" to the four letter last name of Mr. Olds. An employee of the Ford Motor Co., not Henry Ford himself, followed the Olds pattern with the four letter last name of Mr. Ford. Mr. Ford did not learn about it until after the ad appeared. He did not like it and instructed the employee, James Couzens, that the "Fordmobile" name was never to be used again. It never was.

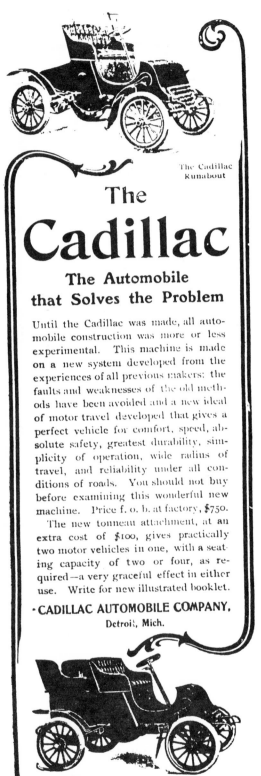

1903 Cadillac

Such things we now take for granted were not even considered on the first Cadillac and other cars of the era, including windshield, top, speedometer, horn, lights, doors, bumpers, shock absorbers, tires with tread, and many other conveniences.

Although this Cadillac engine only had one cylinder, it was made with such precision that it soon earned an excellent reputation which enabled the company to greatly develop and expand.

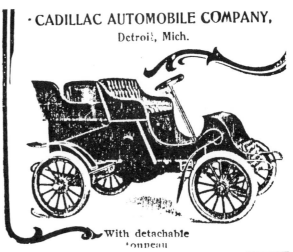

1903 Fordmobile and Cadillac Comparisons

The similarities between the two cars are quite evident. Both companies bought identical bodies from the C. R. Wilson Co. in Detroit. Both illustrations show the rear seat assembly (tonneau) in place. The "detachable tonneau" could be removed or installed in a fairly short time by removing several bolts and lifting it off. The detachable tonneau was the only accessory either company had to offer when these ads appeared. The rear seat compartment had one door in the center of the back of the body; the rear seat passengers sat almost facing each other.

38

This one-cylinder 1903 Rambler runabout, from Kenosha, sold for the same price as the one-cylinder 1903 Cadillac runabout and the two-cylinder Fordmobile runabout. The one cylinder Oldsmobile runabout sold for $650.00. Only the Cadillac and Fordmobile offered a rear seat assembly (for $100.00 more). All four cars had the engine under the seat and the driver on the right. The Oldsmobile and Rambler had tiller steering, while the Cadillac and Fordmobile had steering wheels. Making a hard right turn with the Oldsmobile tiller could be somewhat embarrassing to an overweight passenger as the driver had to move the steering tiller across the passenger's lap.

OLDSMOBILES

THE success of the Oldsmobile is due to its absolute reliability. The working parts are simple, easily understood and all complications are eliminated. For practical use the highest awards in Endurance and Reliability Runs prove this standard Runabout to be ''the Best Thing on Wheels.'' Operated by a single lever from the seat and always under instant control.

The Oldsmobile gives perfect satisfaction on all roads in all kinds of weather; it is build to run *and does it*.

PRICE, $650.00

Write for illustrated book to Dept. Y.

OLDS MOTOR WORKS
DETROIT, MICHIGAN.

The best selling car in this country in 1903 was this Oldsmobile. This curved-dash model is the one referred to in the song as the "Merry Oldsmobile." There was no provision for more than one passenger plus the driver. It was very unusual for a car in this price range to be advertised with an accessory top, shown folded down in this illustration.

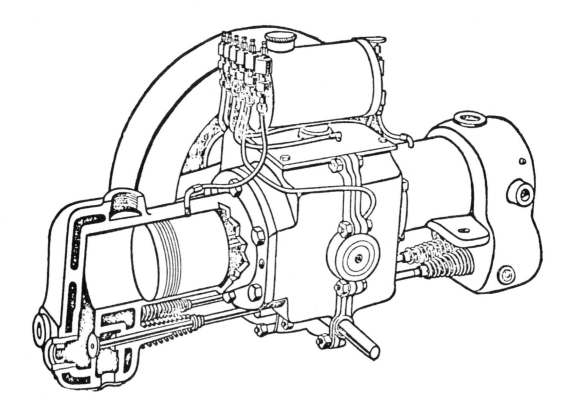

Two Cylinder Ford Engine

Cutaway drawing shows the basic opposed engine which Ford used in its early years. Round tank on top contains oil which flowed by gravity to strategic points of the engine through the various pipes shown in the drawing.

Buick also used a two-cylinder opposed engine in its early years, but it had overhead valves, not the "L" head arrangement shown here on the Ford drawing. Each was an excellent engine for its time.

four letters (like OLDS) but Mr. Ford would have none of the "mobile" idea.

A relative of James Couzens invested $100.00 for one share of stock in the Ford Motor Co. in 1903 and sold the stock back to Henry Ford, after having earned over a quarter of a million dollars. Another early Ford stockholder was Albert Strelow who owned the building on Mack Avenue in Detroit which was Ford's first factory. He put up $5,000.00. Two years later he sold out for 25,000.00, invested that money in a Klondike gold mine and lost it all. Several years later he applied for a job in the Highland Park assembly plant.

The Dodge brothers had gained valuable experience building small automobile parts for several years, then, beginning in 1901, building engines and other parts for Oldsmobile. By 1903, Olds was back on its feet. The Dodge brothers agreed to convert their plant to make mechanical parts for Ford for a 10% interest in the Ford Motor Co. Because of his production experience Horace Dodge made some minor engine and rear axle changes in the original C. H. Wills designs.

Ford didn't sell its first car until July 15, 1903, a month after it started in business. At that time the Ford Motor Co. had only $225.00 in its checking account, so when the check for the Chicago dentist's touring car arrived, it was most welcome. There was, in the early days, no financing a new car purchase; the terms were payment in full with the order for the car.

As irony would have it, both Ford and Cadillac were customers of the C. R. Wilson Co. in Detroit for manufacture of their bodies in 1903; the result was that the Ford and the Cadillac looked identical. To add to the confusion, they sold for exactly the same price, $850.00 for the touring car, with a back seat and $750.00 for a runabout, with no back seat. Both cars were known as Model "A", neither car had any front doors, and each had only one rear door in the center of the rear seats. Neither car had a windshield, or a top, or a horn, or lights of any kind. The Fordmobile had a two-cylinder engine while the Cadillac had a one-cylinder engine. There were other chassis and running gear differences, but both had the engine under the front seat and both had a planetary two-speed transmission with a single driving chain to the rear axle.

Of course, both the Fordmobile and the Cadillac were also quite similar to other cars built in the midwest of that era, some still well known today, and others no longer remembered. In addition to the Cadillac and Fordmobile offerings, one could also buy a one-cylinder curved dash Merry Oldsmobile in Detroit for $650.00 and the Rambler from Kenosha, which also had a one cylinder engine, and sold for $750.00.

David Buick And Henry Ford Comparisons

David Buick's financial bankers were getting impatient with him for not making money the same way Henry Ford's backers did the previous year. Mr. Buick's backers wanted to keep the company so they could sell it as a going business, not like Mr. Ford's second set of "angels" did a year earlier.

The Buick Motor Co. was formed on May 19, 1903. It was Mr. Buick's third automobile company. Mr. Ford's first venture into the automobile business, the Detroit Automobile Co., as well as his second, the Henry Ford Co. both went under because the financial backers pulled out their money. The Buick Motor Co. was incorporated a little less than a month earlier than the Ford Motor Co. In both cases, the men whose names were on their respective front doors had no money invested. Only their experience, mechanical know-how and determination to succeed were what they had to offer. Mr. Ford was more fortunate in having an excellent man to look after the books and money, James Couzens, than was Mr. Buick. Both had brilliant engineers; Mr. Ford had C. H. Wills and Mr. Buick had Walter Marr. Both had designed two-cylinder engines for their respective cars and both engines were excellent for the times.

By the end of the summer of 1903 it was obvious to the Briscoe brothers, Mr. Buick's "angels", that from the way they were going, things were not going to succeed. A fellow in nearby Flint, Michigan wanted to get into automobile manufacturing. He already had a factory in Flint and was doing quite well making buggies, but he foresaw that the automobile would replace horse-drawn vehicles in the near future. His name was James Whiting. He and the Briscoe's found each other, and the Buick Motor Co. was sold and moved to Flint.

Apparently, the only car actually made in Detroit was the one delivered to the Briscoe's in early 1903 by the Buick Manufacturing Co. before it was re-organized into the Buick Motor Co. For a while the Buick Motor Co. made only motors (engines) and sold them for use as marine and stationary engines and even to be used by other manufacturers of automobiles. The brilliant engineer, Walter Marr, came to Flint with the Buick Motor Co. Mr. Buick was the secretary of the company.

In the summer of 1903, while still having money invested in Buick, Ben Briscoe put money behind Jonathan Maxwell, and would eventually build the Maxwell-Briscoe car. Mr. Maxwell's association with the "Northern" car lasted less than a year.

The Dusenberg Name First Appears In The Auto Business

Up in Kenosha, Wisconsin, the Jeffery Co. hired a young man as a test driver for their Rambler cars; his name was Fred Dusenberg.

Packard Moves From Warren, Ohio To Detroit

In the summer of 1903, the Packard Motor Co. moved from Warren, Ohio to Detroit where rail and water shipping and skilled labor were more available.

The Panama Canal Is Begun

Another piece of transportation history began this year for the United States and took eleven years to complete. That was the Panama Canal, a project which had been abandoned by the French.

Orville And Wilbur Quietly Succeed Before Christmas

Still one more piece of transportation took place in 1903. The Ford Motor Co. was about six months old when Henry Ford bought his first dress suit for $65.00; when Cadillac had been producing cars about nine months; when Rambler had been producing cars for about a year and a half; and when Olds had been producing cars for about six years. Of course I am speaking of the Wright brothers' flight at Kitty Hawk on December 17. The Wright brothers were from Dayton, Ohio and, like the early automobile manufacturers, used a basic internal combustion engine for their power.

Sharples Tubular Separators

GREAT SEPARATOR CONTEST

Held Dec. 17, 1903, at Minnesota Dairymen's Convention

Our Claim

We will place a Sharples Tubular beside any other separator, and guarantee the Tubular to cut in half any record for clean skimming the other machine can make.

The Challenge

Three competitors, each beaten hundreds of times singly, band together and enter a contest against the Sharples Tubular. Providing the "combine-of-three" are allowed to furnish the milk. Providing the "combine-of-three" dictate temperature of milk. Providing the "combine-of-three" dictate quantity of milk. Providing the "combine of three" run three machines, and if any one leaves less than double the fat of the Sharples Tubular, they win. The "combine-of-three" select cold, hard-skimming cows' milk (62° to 70°) 200 lbs. at a run.

The Result

Sharples Tubular		.05
"The Combine of Three" {	Alpha De Laval	.175
	United States	.225
	Empire	.450

The report was signed by Robert Crickmore, Creamery Mgr.; A. W. Trow, Pres., Minn. Dairymen's Ass'n.; and E. J. Henry, Babcock Tester Expert, the judges mutually agreed upon. Write for complete report and Catalog E-145.

THE SHARPLES CO.
Chicago, Ill.

P. M. SHARPLES
West Chester, Pa.

December 17, 1903

Orville and Wilbur Wright didn't know what was going on up in Minnesota any more than these people knew how history was being made at Kitty Hawk on the very same day!

1904

Mr. Olds Leaves The Olds Motor Works

Early in 1904 Mr. Olds disagreed with the family named Smith about the future of the Olds Motor Works. The Smith's had the money behind Olds so their decision was final whether Mr. Olds happened to agree with it or not. The curved dash Merry Oldsmobile with its one-cylinder engine was the best selling car in this country at the time. Its price was $650.00. Mr. Olds wanted the company to concentrate on low-priced cars, reasoning that there were more people with a few dollars than there were with a lot of dollars. It was time to start designing and experimenting with a replacement for the little one-cylinder car which could only carry two people. The Smith family, father and two sons, wanted to concentrate on large expensive cars aimed at the wealthy because they reasoned that there would be more profit in expensive cars, and that the name would have more prestige. Mr. Olds left the company and quickly found others to put up money. Soon he was making a car with the name formed by his initials, R.E.O., and concentrated on small cars for several years. As we shall see later, the Smith family's decision led to Oldsmobile's downfall. The Olds Motor Works decided to move back to Lansing after much financial persuasion from the City Fathers of Lansing.

Henry Leland Joins Cadillac Full Time

The first Cadillac's were having a few chassis problems. Nothing was wrong with the engines and transmissions supplied by Mr. Leland's machine shop, but with the other chassis components. It became obvious that a much more experienced hand was needed in running Cadillac. Again Henry Leland was called upon. Until then, Leland had strictly been Cadillac's exclusive engine and transmission supplier. He was aware of the chassis problems and could see that if they were not solved he would have no one to buy his engines and transmissions. In late 1904 he agreed to take over Cadillac as General Manager that amounted to absorbing the Leland and Faulkner Machine Shop into Cadillac, with exchanges of cash and stock.

Studebaker Joins With Garford

In South Bend, the Studebaker Company had been in business for over fifty years as builders of wagons and carriages and a full line of horse-drawn vehicles. They had been building a few of their own electric cars for two years. Now, Studebaker entered into an agreement with the Garford Company in Elyria, Ohio, to build bodies. Garford shipped all the mechanical parts for the cars to Studebaker that assembled everything and installed its own bodies. The car was sold as Studebaker-Garford and was sold mostly through the existing network of horse-drawn vehicle dealers as the electric cars had been for the past two years. By this time Studebaker also had some manufacturing operations in Detroit.

Buick Calls On W. C. Durant For Help

This year turned out to be the start of something big for the Buick Motor Company and the City of Flint. Mr. Buick's boss was Mr. Whiting and Mr. Buick pestered him enough to get

1904 Cadillac Touring Car

It had a one-cylinder engine under the front seat and cranked from the left side of the car. Oil and water tanks were under the hood. Top and lights and windshield were accessories.

Entrance to the rear seat was by the single rear door, visible here in the center of the rear of the body.

Source: *National Auto History Collection*
of the Detroit Public Library

Robert C. Faulkner and Henry M. Leland

Robert C. Faulkner, on the left, and Henry M. Leland, on the right, in the office of their Detroit machine shop. Roll top desks, wire waste baskets, and bare hardwood floors were in style at the time. The clear bare light bulb over Mr. Leland's desk must have produced quite a glare.

Source: *National Auto History Collection
of the Detroit Public Library*

1904 Buick

The first Buick was the Model "B" of 1904.

48

the go ahead to make a complete car, not just to make engines for other people. The first car was ready in early July and made a test run to Detroit and back without any problems. The driver was Walter Marr and Mr. Buick's son was the passenger. A Flint doctor got the first Buick actually completed, presumed to be the same chassis as the one used on the test run to Detroit and back.

Over a dozen other people ordered cars and it was about now that owner Whiting realized that he had a tiger by the tail. The details and expense of running an automobile manufacturing company were considerably more complicated than those of the carriage company Whiting had been used to. He wasn't able to handle it as they kept on building and attempting to fill orders.

About this time a partner of one of the other carriage makers in Flint learned in a round about way that the Buick Motor Company needed help. He was William C. Durant. Durant asked the Buick Motor Co. for a car to use as a demonstrator. They taught him how to drive it, and drive it is just what he did. For the next several weeks Durant drove on the good roads and the bad roads, getting stuck a few times and breaking down a few times. The overall impression was good and Mr. Durant agreed to take over running the Buick Motor Company and Mr. Whiting stayed with the company. Mr. Whiting and Mr. Durant were partners in Buick, yet competitors in the carriage business for a while.

The Hot Dog Becomes Popular

A new invention called the "hot dog" was served at the St. Louis Exposition of 1904. Legend has it that the sausage on a roll was originally named a hot daschund but that a reporter for St. Louis newspaper could not spell too well and "hot dog" is what it has been called ever since.

1905

Cadillac And Ford No Longer Looked Identical

By now Cadillac and Ford had both evolved to the point where each had a little hood out in front of the car and no longer looked identical, as did their original models two years earlier. Each still used its original engine, the one-cylinder Cadillac and the two-cylinder Ford. Each also had added a four-cylinder model by now. Advertising of both Ford and Cadillac, and of other cars too, by this time pictured their respective cars with the rear side doors open so that it could be readily seen how easy it was to get into the rear seat. This was the transition period when the rear entrance tonneau was being replaced by the side entrance type. In another couple of years, all cars built in this country would be the side-entrance type. The reason cars still did not have front doors will be discussed in a later chapter.

Durant Expands The Buick Facilities

When Mr.Durant took over Buick in late 1904, he saw that one of the things needed right away was more space and better organization. It just so happened that the Durant-Dort

Rear Entrance Tonneau

Auto makers were not certain whether gasoline or electric or steam was the proper
method of motive power in 1903. The International Motor Car Co. covered the field with all
three. Note that the car in the drawing on the left has no side doors. Also a door for the driver
would have made it impossible for him to use the brake and gearshift levers, mounted on the
right, outside the frame.

The drawing of the 1904 Packard, on the right, shows the single rear step and single door
in the center. Rear seat passengers sat almost facing each other.

50

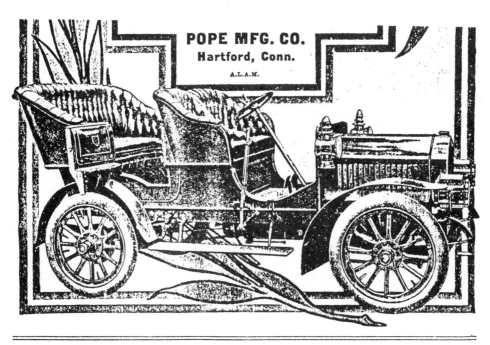

POPE MFG. CO.
Hartford, Conn.
A.L.A.M.

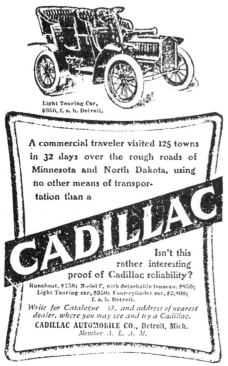

Light Touring Car,
$950, f. o. b. Detroit.

A commercial traveler visited 125 towns in 32 days over the rough roads of Minnesota and North Dakota, using no other means of transportation than a

CADILLAC

Isn't this rather interesting proof of Cadillac reliability?

Runabout, $750; Model C, with detachable tonneau, $850; Light Touring car, $950; Four-cylinder car, $2,800; f. o. b. Detroit.

Write for Catalogue D, and address of nearest dealer, where you may see and try a Cadillac.

CADILLAC AUTOMOBILE CO., Detroit, Mich.
Member A. L. A. M.

The "rear entrance tonneau" body was rapidly losing favor due to its extreme inconvenience. These two manufacturers advertised their 1905 cars with the doors open to show how easy it was to enter or leave the rear seat.

Because of tradition, no one considered front doors at this time. This came from the horse and wagon days when teamsters sometimes stood up to guide the horses and needed plenty of room to work the reins. It wasn't until about 1910 that front doors were seriously considered.

Carriage Co. had an unused factory building down in Jackson, Michigan. The Jackson factory was reopened and used to assemble the complete cars, the component parts being shipped in from Flint. The Jackson factory was used as late as 1912 to assemble the small Buick trucks, which still had the two-cylinder engine. A new factory was begun in 1905 for Buick in Flint.

Henry Ford Buys Out One Of His Backers

Henry Ford had one of his early disagreements, for which he was to become famous during the remaining 42 years of his life. One of his major financial backers two years earlier had been coal dealer Malcomson and this was one of the early incidents to arouse the temper of the very strange personality of Henry Ford, now age 41. He settled this argument the way he settled most of them, by using money to get his way. He simply got Mr. Malcomson out of his life by buying all of his stock in the company.

Dodge's Still Making Parts For Ford

The Dodge brothers were still concentrating all their efforts upon making the mechanical parts for the Ford Motor Co., and both the Dodge and Ford companies were making money.

Ransom Olds Making Cars Again

Mr. Olds, now 40, was head of the company making the small REO cars in Lansing.

Henry Leland's Last New Car

Henry Leland, general manager of Cadillac, took delivery of a new one-cylinder Cadillac with a coupé body. He never got another new car although he lived a very active life for 27 more years. He referred to the car as "Osceola" out of respect for the Chief of the Seminole tribe for whom he had a deep admiration.

Swiss Born Louis Chevrolet Comes To The U.S.A.

Louis Chevrolet had graduated from racing bicycles to racing automobiles and came to the United States in 1905 to race them. By the end of the year he had beaten the famous Barney Oldfield.

Walter Chrysler Still In Railroading

Walter Chrysler, 30, was now superintendent of Motive Power for the Chicago Great Western Railway.

Charles Nash Still In The Carriage Business

Charles Nash, 41, was Superintendent of Production for the Durant-Dort Carriage Works, the largest such business in Flint.

Source: *National Auto History Collection
of the Detroit Public Library*

1905 REO Touring Car

This car was made by a new company headed by Mr. Ransom Eli Olds, using his initials, shortly after he resigned from the Olds Motor Works. Mr. Olds wanted to modernize the Olds Motor Works, but to keep on building small cars. The Smith family, who controlled the Olds money, wanted to make big cars only, so Mr. Olds resigned and formed the REO company. History proved Mr. Olds correct as his REO company prospered for many years, eventually concentrating on trucks only. The Olds Motor Works lost money by making big cars almost exclusively and was on the way to financial disaster when the Smith family sold the Olds Motor Works to Mr. Durant's new General Motors on November 12, 1908.

Charles Kettering Makes National Cash Register Famous

Charles Kettering, 29, working for the National Cash Register Co. in Dayton, Ohio, developed a small, but very powerful electric motor for its size to electrify the cash register.

Roy Chapin Leaves Oldsmobile For Other Auto Ventures

Roy Chapin, 24, resigned as sales manager of Oldsmobile where he had worked his way up in four years. He, and a partner, were able to get a third man to put up money for a car that they wanted to build the following year.

1906

An Extremely Close Call For Roy Chapin And His Sister

In the spring, Roy Chapin and his sister Daisy had been on a combination vacation and business trip in California. They headed home from Oakland on April 18 and were on the last train that left San Francisco before the earthquake.

C. H. Wills Of Ford Motor Co. Makes Metallurgy Breakthrough

It was this year when C. H. Wills, the metallurgist and Henry Ford's "sparring partner" of about four years earlier, made an important discovery. He was still working for Ford. The discovery was a method to produce "vanadium steel" at a reasonable price and in large quantities. Wills did not invent the process, as vanadium steel was well known for its strength and light weight, but at great production expense. What Mr. Wills did was to make it practical for automobile usage, which meant large quantities, at low enough cost to be able to be used in a low-priced car. The extra strong steel meant that smaller, thinner and therefore lighter weight parts could be used for axles and steering parts, for engine parts, and for many other mechanical parts of the car.

British "Dewar Cup" Awarded To The Stanley

Sir Thomas Dewar of England offered the "Dewar Cup" to whoever drove the mile in the shortest time. The Dewar Cup was won by a Stanley steam-racer clocked at 127 miles an hour, over two miles a minute, on Ormond Beach, Florida, and driven by Fred Marriott, a Stanley employee. This same year of 1906 was the most successful one in the history of the Durant-Dort Carriage Company in Flint, which had been in business since 1886.

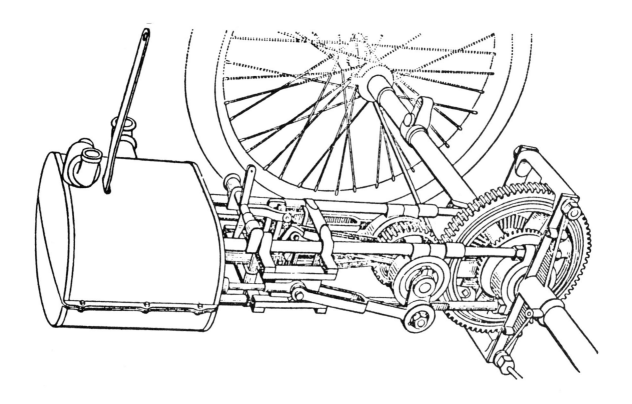

Stanley Engine And Axle

Cutaway drawing shows the basic design of the Stanley two cylinder steam engine built right on the rear axle. With some modifications for speed, this is the same basic design which drove the Stanley racer over 120 miles an hour in 1906.

Source: *National Auto History Collection of the Detroit Public Library*

Fred Marriott poses for a photo in the Stanley steam racer in 1906 on the hard sand at Ormond Beach, Florida. This car, with less than 25 moving parts in its engine, went over 120 miles an hour during these speed runs.

1906, Fred Marriott taking practice runs on the hard sand at Ormond Beach prior to setting the over 120 M.P.H. record. As this action photo indicates, steam was exhausted directly into the atmosphere from the engine.

1907

Ford Has Six Cylinder Engine Problems

This was still a time of experimenting with what the public would buy. People would buy almost anything regardless of how poorly designed it was or how poorly suited it was to their particular needs. The same is still true today. The different car makers, if they wanted to survive, could only experiment to try to catch the public's fancy with well-made cars. The really poorly designed cars didn't stay in production too long.

Buick made a cheap and a medium-priced model but only a few high-priced cars. Oldsmobile still made the low-priced one-cylinder car, but was concentrating its efforts on making only high-priced models, and was not selling many of them. Cadillac was still making its small one-cylinder car, as well as high-priced models, and because of their better quality, Cadillac was doing much better than Oldsmobile.

Ford went off the deep end, and in 1906 and 1907 made a six-cylinder car, which one still had to crank, the Model "K". The Model "K" was not all that well-engineered and Ford could not get the vibration out of the engine; so this model was only made for about a year and a half. The advertising for the Model "K" stressed that it had a six-cylinder engine and that a "six" was the up and coming thing for a high class car, even saying "Don't Be a Year Behind-er" and adding that buying anything other than a six was "buying a car already a year out of date".

The Model "K" was priced at $2,800.00 while the highest priced Cadillac of 1907, which had a four-cylinder engine, was priced at $2,500.00. So then, at least, the Ford, which originally began at the same price as the Cadillac, when each had only one model, now had its highest priced model costing more than the highest priced Cadillac by $300.00. Since the Model "K" was not a financial success for Ford because of the vibration in the six-cylinder engine, Mr. Ford never again allowed a "six" to be made until 1941, when he was not very active in the company any more due to advanced age. Ford still made the Model "N" and the Model "R" in 1907, both of which were four-cylinder cars.

Henry Leland Brings Even More Precision To Cadillac

It was about this time when Henry Leland brought to Cadillac a new and even finer way of assuring precision. This was with the Johannson gauges. These were a master set of ultra-precision gauges and were used to check and double check the gauges that were actually used in the shop. The master set was kept at a controlled temperature and was just used to check the shop gauges. In the shop a part was made to fit exactly into the proper gauge or it was rejected. Each piece of machine work was checked twice. Each machine part had to fit only the one, but not the other. If it also fit the "too small" (or "too large") gauge, the part was scrapped. The "too small" or "too large" gauges were less than one/one-thousandth of an inch different than the proper gauge. It entailed quite an expense, but it helped give Cadillac a good name in those days. Within a few years, the entire machine tool industry became familiar with the process.

J. P. Morgan And The Financial Panic Of 1907

In 1907, a financial panic was deliberately caused by the wealthy J. Pierpont Morgan just to prove to everyone that he, himself, personally could cause such a panic because he was so wealthy and therefore so powerful. All he did was to demand that those who owed him money

1906-07 Ford Model "K"

Source: *National Auto History Collection of the Detroit Public Library*

Both of these ads appeared in 1907. The second paragraph of the Cadillac shows the price for their most expensive car, the Model H to be $300.00 cheaper than Ford's most expensive model.

Source: *National Auto History Collection
of the Detroit Public Library*

1906-1912 International High Wheeler

International made this same basic vehicle from approximately 1906 to approximately 1912. It was one of several makes of vehicles known as "high wheelers" for obvious reasons. Tall wheels were about the same size as wagon wheels and were supposed to give ample ground clearance on the ruts the wagons of the era had to use. On this particular vehicle the rear seat assembly was an accessory, it could be removed permitting the vehicle to be used as a light truck.

You could buy a Sears high wheeler through the Sears catalog. Other brands were also available by mail order; most were shipped in crates with "full instructions". For those not mechanically inclined, the local blacksmith could assemble the kit into a finished vehicle.

pay at once. This is known as "calling a note". If the debtor refused or could not pay, J. P. Morgan simply took over or repossessed the collateral on which the note had originally been based. He had seen to it that this provision of repossession was legally written into every situation where he loaned out his money through his Bankers Trust Co. bank in New York City.

During the panic of 1907, Mr. Durant was blessed with either tremendous foresight, or tremendous ignorance, as he kept the Buick factories running at full speed while other manufacturers slowed down production as sales dropped. When the panic suddenly ended, Buick was the only car maker with a large supply of cars on hand to sell. Mr. Durant had applied to the Buick company the same principle that had made his carriage company so profitable, that is, to buy all suppliers and therefore get all parts at cost.

Now with Buick, he owned or controlled suppliers of axles, wheels, engines, spark plugs, and many other components. Thanks to a suggestion by Ben Briscoe, Durant now began to envision an automobile "holding company", whereby all the automobile makers would be owned by just a few concerns, and together they would never run out of parts to build their cars. He talked to Mr. Smith and his sons who now owned Oldsmobile; to Mr. Olds who now owned REO; also to representatives of Ford, Pierce-Arrow, Packard, Thomas, Peerless, Stoddard-Dayton, and to his old friend Ben Briscoe of Maxwell-Briscoe.

Fred Marriott Returns To Ormond Beach With The Stanley Racer

In January, a Stanley steam-racer was again on the hard sand at Ormond Beach to set another record of the straight measured mile. The driver was again Fred Marriott, a Stanley employee. As permitted by the rules, Marriott started nine miles up from the starting line so that by the time he reached the starting line, he was going at full speed over three miles a minute (180 M.P.H.). Unfortunately, there was a slight dip in the sand which caused the speeding racer to become airborne for the next 100 feet. Marriott fully recovered from all his injuries, but the Stanley's decided that a loving cup prize was not worth the risk of injury and so they ceased their racing activities.

That record of 180 miles an hour remained unbroken for over forty years, or until after World War II, for a car of that weight, 2200 pounds. The engine of that car is now in the Smithsonian in Washington. It has two cylinders and less than 25 moving parts!

1908

David Buick Leaves The Buick Motor Co.

This turned out to be another very eventful year in the United States in the automobile business. Mr. Buick resigned from the Buick Motor Co. because he was too slow and plodding for the wheeling and dealing activities of the organization as run by Mr. Durant. Mr. Durant personally saw to it that Mr. Buick had a good bit of cash and a good bit of Buick Motor Co. stock. After leaving Mr. Durant's employ, Mr. Buick tried and failed at an oil company venture out West, a small manufacturing plant back in Detroit, another automobile company already on its last legs, and Florida real estate during the land boom of the 1920's. Finally, he

1907 Stanley Roadster

Car is being backed out of a parking space. Steam is being exhausted into the atmosphere directly from the engine. The gentleman, on the right, is driving. The two-cylinder engine is mounted horizontally directly in front of the rear axle. Later model stanley's had this exhaust steam go through a system of pipes and a condenser which converted the steam into hot water so that it could be used over and over again.

Source: *National Auto History Collection
of the Detroit Public Library*

1908 Stanley Roadster

Source: *National Auto History Collection
of the Detroit Public Library*

President T. R. In The White House Car

President Theodore Roosevelt in the official White House car, a White Steamer. It was a regular production car, with no special equipment for presidential use. The driver, George H. Robinson, was an employee of the Quartermaster Corps. He was a very experienced automobile driver and his distinguished service in the Quartermaster Corps earned him the reward of being the presidential chauffeur. The same car and driver also served William Howard Taft when he became President. Mr. Robinson returned to Quartermaster Corps duties at the end of the Taft administration.

Source: *National Auto History Collection
of the Detroit Public Library*

1909 White Steamer Chassis

The Chassis only was at an automobile show. The engine was under the hood and the boiler, or steam generator, was under the front seat. Since White used a "flash" type boiler, there was not built up steam pressure to cause concern.

What may look like a second steering wheel is actually the throttle control. The larger wheel is the steering wheel. Turning the smaller wheel clockwise fed more steam to the engine to go faster. You could grip the steering wheel normally and control the speed by moving the throttle wheel with your thumb, never taking your hand from the steering.

Source: *National Auto History Collection*
of the Detroit Public Library

1908 White Steamer

was an instructor at a Detroit trade school teaching boys how to repair cars. He died, forgotten and broke, in 1929.

Walter Chrysler Buys His First Car

Mr. Walter Chrysler, the railroad man, visited the Chicago Automobile show and bought a $5,000.00 Locomobile touring car with $700.00 down and a $4,300.00 loan from a Chicago bank. Mr. Chrysler had the car shipped home to Iowa, dismantled it in the barn to learn how it was supposed to work, then made sketches and put it all back together. The first time he actually drove the car under its own power, a neighbor's garden got in the way!

Louis Chevrolet Goes To Work For The Buick Motor Co.

Mr. Louis Chevrolet came to the Buick Motor Co. as a race driver for the Buick factory team. His brother, Arthur became the chauffeur for Mr. Durant. Their other brother, Gaston, was also a race driver but did not go to work for Buick as the other brothers did.

Another Industry Develops "Pressed Steel"

About this time "pressed steel" came into wide usage in the manufacture of automobiles and other items. Steel was "pressed" by putting a piece of sheet steel in a hydraulic press capable of exerting tremendous pressure so as to form the steel into the desired shape. The pressing of steel in this manner allowed it to keep its original strength.

Until that time bath tubs were made in several sections, were soldered together, and then had the porcelain applied. The "pressed steel" process meant that the tub could be made in one piece and was therefore not subject to leakage at a soldered joint. But a totally different industry was actually responsible for developing pressed steel, its product being similar in size and shape to the bath tub. This product too, had to remain perfectly air and moisture tight. Pressed steel was developed by the casket industry.

Roy Chapin Woos Hugh Chalmers From National Cash Register

Mr. Roy Chapin and Mr. Howard Coffin, of the one-year-old Thomas-Detroit Company, brought in a new sales manager, Mr. Hugh Chalmers, former sales manager for the National Cash Register Co. of Dayton, Ohio. Just a couple of years earlier, Mr. Charles Kettering's invention for making cash registers operate electrically greatly contributed to the company's huge success and made Mr. Chalmers' job much easier by having a new and very high quality product. We will see later that Mr. Chapin would soon form the Hudson Motor Car Co.; Mr. Chalmers would soon have a car with his name which would eventually be a part of the Chrysler Corporation. Mr. Kettering would later contribute very many ideas and inventions to the automobile industry.

Dr. Hills Sells The First Buick

Dr. Herbert H. Hills, who had bought the first Buick in 1904, and had driven it on his rounds, sold it in 1908 to a superintendent at the Buick factory, one George Weber. Then Mr. Weber drove the car until 1911 when he jacked it up and sold off the various parts; that is to say he "junked" it and now all historical significance with that car is gone forever.

Source: *National Auto History Collection
of the Detroit Public Library*

1908 Thomas Flyer in the New York To Paris Race

The race started in New York City, went westward across the United States, then by ship across the Pacific, then across Siberia, Russia, and Europe to Paris. A movie made several years ago, "The Great Race", with Tony Curtis, Keenan Wynn, and Jack Lemon, was based, rather loosely, on this race. The U. S. entry, the Thomas in this photo, did, in fact win the race. The car itself is still in existence, having been restored in the Reno shops of the late William Harrah.

The photo shows the car, somewhat modified for the race, as it encountered normal road conditions encountered everywhere outside those cities which had paved streets.

Source: *National Auto History Collection of the Detroit Public Library*

1908 Buick Model "10"

This was Durant's competitor to the small, low-priced Model "T" Ford. The car shown in this illustration was not equipped with a windshield or top, both of which were available as extra cost accessories. Doors were not even available. The Model 10 Buick was produced during 1908-09-10. Unlike Ford, Buick also had higher-priced models. After Durant lost control of General Motors in the late 1910, the new leaders did not want to be associated with this low-priced car.

Young Lady Driving A Model 10 Buick

This is the car which William C. Durant hoped would challenge the Model "T" Ford, was only on the market a short time. The Buick Model 10 was probably the slightly better of the two cars, but Buick had several other models. Ford concentrated all its production and selling efforts on its one and only car, the Model "T". In addition, Buick and General Motors had financial problems due to expanding too fast. New directors at G.M. decided that they didn't want to be associated with a low-priced car, so the Model 10 Buick was dropped after the 1910 production run. It had been built in 1908, 1909, and 1910.

The big brass headlights shown on this car were standard equipment, as was the light gray paint. The top, shown here folded down, was an accessory, and so was a windshield which the original owner of this car did not buy. It is quite obvious that this is a posed picture, as the undersides of the fenders, and even the tires, are clean which would not have been possible if the car had been driven on the "road" shown here.

General Motors Is Secretly Formed

A set of circumstances of the deepest secrecy was coming together in late September. For about a year and a half Mr. Durant of Buick had been manipulating, talking consolidation and attempting to hatch his "holding company". Through hemming and hawing and foot shuffling, Mr. Olds at REO declined to join with anyone less successful than himself. Henry Ford took this opportunity to attempt to stop the consolidation because he knew he would have to share the spotlight with Mr. Durant. He chose to say that he wanted eight million dollars in cash for the Ford Motor Co. He thought this would stop all activities because he knew that Mr. Durant could not possibly raise that much cash at that time. Also, late in the year, Ford began tooling up for its new model for 1909, the Model "T". The Model "S" was the 1908 Ford. There were only about 300 Model "T" Fords built during the very last part of 1908, and they were all known as 1909 models.

There had also been attempts to interest the J. P. Morgan owned bank in New York in the "holding company" consolidation plan, but when the bank learned Mr. Durant would control everything, they said "NO"! The result of all this was that in *VERY* deep secrecy, General Motors was founded with only $2,000.00 on September 16, 1908. Two weeks later, on September 28, the original two thousand was raised to twelve and a half million. Three days later, on October 1, 1908, General Motors "bought" Buick for three and three quarter million with both G. M. and Buick being controlled by Durant; then on November 12, 1908, the week after William Howard Taft was elected President of the United States, Oldsmobile was bought by General Motors for just over three million.

Some of those who had originaly talked with Mr. Durant — consolidation had been Benjamin Briscoe's idea, not Durant's — decided to form the United States Motors Corporation. Another combine was also formed in 1908 with Studebaker and E.M.F. All three of those holding companies, General Motors, U.S. Motors, and E.M.F. — Studebaker eventually went broke.

British "Dewar Trophy" Awarded To Cadillac

Over a period of time Mr. Leland bought out all the other Cadillac stockholders so that by 1908 he and his son owned it all. They were still making the one-cylinder Cadillac in 1908 (its last year) when the British distributor decided to get a contest going which he knew Cadillac would win because of its extra precision and interchangeable-parts ideas.

The English distributor had the Royal Automobile Club set up a contest with the object being to take three cars from the English distributor's stock. The three cars were taken to the new Brooklands Race Track in England where each was driven around the track until it had exactly 100 miles on it, then all three cars were completely disassembled, using only ordinary hand tools, under the direction of the Royal Automobile Club. All the parts were completely mixed up as the cars were taken apart so that it was impossible to tell which part came from which car. Then, about 75 or 80 parts were taken out of the big pile and the Cadillac distributor furnished new parts to replace them. The mechanics re-assembled the three cars again using ordinary hand tools. No files and no "special fitting" were permitted.

When all three cars were re-assembled out of the pile of parts, two cars started on the first pull of the crank, the other car took two pulls on the crank. The Royal Automobile Club was so impressed by this performance that they awarded Cadillac the Dewar Trophy. For the first time a company outside England received the trophy. Sir Thomas Dewar had established the trophy to be awarded to the most distinguished automobile of that particular year. This award was established in addition to the Dewar cup and went to who ever drove the mile in the shortest time. The Stanley Steamer won in 1906.

Locomobile and Maxwell Cars in Dealer Showroom

The three cars on the left side of this photo are the prestige Locomobile, and the others are low and medium priced Maxwells. Dual dealerships, such as this, were tolerated then, as now, by both auto manufacturers as long as the other brand handled by the dealer was not a direct competitor. The Locomobile limousine, on the extreme left edge of this picture, very likely cost more than any three of the Maxwell's pictured here.

1909

Oakland Joins General Motors

Early in the year, Mr. Durant went shopping to buy small existing automobile-related companies which were making good products. He found Mr. Murphy, owner of the Oakland Motor Car Co. in nearby Pontiac, Michigan. The car was good but the company had money problems and Mr. Durant and Mr. Murphy became personal friends. Mr. Murphy sold the Oakland Motor Car Co. to General Motors in exchange for cash and stock in General Motors, which was the normal Durant way of doing business. Mr. Murphy was to stay on and continue to run the Oakland Motor Car Co. Just a few weeks later, however, Mr. Murphy died unexpectedly. The Murphy family received the benefits of the sale.

General Motors Finally Buys Cadillac

Mr. Durant's negotiations with Henry Leland to buy Cadillac for General Motors were finally completed in the summer of 1909. He had not procrastinated. Durant could have bought Cadillac for a million dollars less than the five and three quarter million he wound up paying. It was the largest single financial transaction that Detroit had seen up until that time. One of the terms of the sale was that the Leland's, father and son, would still run the company with a free hand and receive handsome salaries plus a percentage of the profits.

Model "T" Ford Brakes And Steering Explained

Early in the year, Henry Ford discovered that he had to cheapen the quality of the Model "T" if he was going to make a profit. The first 2500 cars bore only a slight mechanical resemblance to the remainder of the production run. For some unknown reason, it caught on. The Model "T" Ford was out of date and unsafe when the first one was built. Every other manufacturer who had used a planetary transmission had either replaced it or was phasing it out by 1909.

The unsafe Model "T" items were the steering mechanism and the brakes. The steering gear was located directly under the steering wheel which resulted in considerable lost motion and bending between the steering gear and the front wheels they were supposed to steer. The result was that in the muddy roads of the time, or snow, sand, or even a deep puddle of water, you could not be sure where the car was going, due to all the lost motion between the front wheels and the steering gear. On other cars, the steering gear was bolted to the car frame in the engine compartment at the front of the frame, which was half way between the front wheels and the steering wheel. The only possibility of lost motion for other cars was between the steering gear and the front wheels. There was no lost motion inside the steering column (as on the Model "T" Ford). The result was that the driver had a much better idea where his car would be going when he encountered adverse road conditions, all of which made other cars safer to drive.

The Model "T" Ford brakes were unsafe for two reasons: (1) they were located inside the transmission, and (2) the amount of braking surface was too small. By being inside the transmission, all of the rear drive-line parts of the car took part in the braking action and, if one of them failed, or broke (not all the parts were vanadium steel), the car had no way of

Fig. 456. Sun-and-Planet Gears of the Ford Steering Gear.

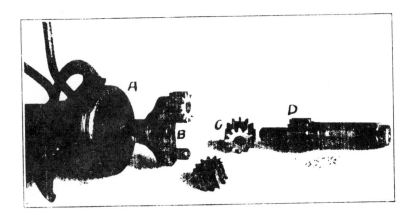

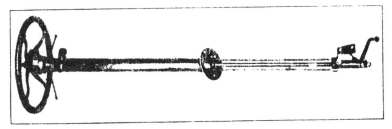

Fig. 455. Ford Steering-Gear Assembly.

Model "T" Ford Steering Gear

The lower photo of the steering gear assembly shows how the bottom bracket is bolted to the frame with just a ball and socket to connect to the tie rods. Other views show the reduction gears just beneath the steering wheel. Other cars had the steering gear box bolted to the frame, giving much more stability.

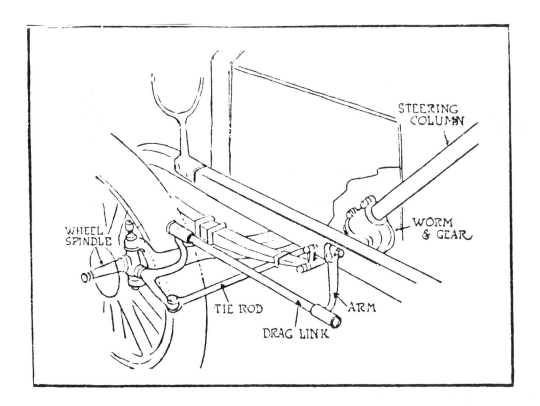

Steering Gear Mounting

Phantom view of steering gear arrangement that was used by all auto manufacturers in this country, except Ford during the Model "T" era. As shown here, the gear box was mounted on the frame itself which, unlike the Ford system, prevented the chance of dangerous lost motion between the steering wheel and the front tires.

The spring suspension shown here is also the type used by every U.S. manufacturer during the 1920's, except Ford. This system meant considerably less sway than the Ford had, where only one front spring was used which was only bolted in the center of the frame.

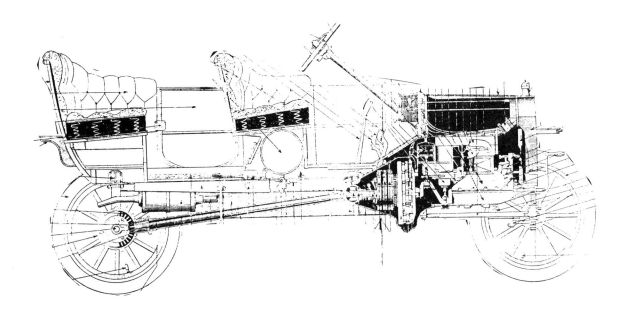

Cutaway view of an early Model "T" Ford. The brake drum and band, shown here by the arrow, were inside the transmission and had to work against the universal joint, drive shaft, differential gears, bearings, and axles. If any of these parts were to fail, not all were vanadium steel, the driver had no way of stopping the car. Other manufacturers had the brake on the transmission on one model or another, but only for a short time. Ford built 15 million cars for more than 18 years with this same arrangement.

Royal External Emergency Brake for Fords

$4.50 PAIR

Replaces internal expansion brakes in rear wheels of Ford. Neither old brakes nor wheels need be removed.

Quickly attached—no drilling required. Lined with Raybestos; guaranteed for one year. Made of rolled steel 8¼x1¼, covered with rust resisting compound. Brake tension kept tight by adjusting nut.

It is an emergency brake that will hold car on the steepest hill.

Price, per pair.... $4.50; per doz. pairs, $51.00

The emergency brakes on the Model "T" Fords were all but non-existent. This company made this arrangement to bolt on the outside of the rear drums. Since the standard Ford emergency brake was ineffective on the inside of the drums, it was not disturbed.

being stopped by the driver. Other manufacturers of the time installed one brake on each rear wheel, which meant that if a drive-line part failed or broke, the brakes could still be used to stop the car, since the brakes were acting on the rear drums which were bolted to each rear wheel. A few other car makers of the era used a drive-line or transmission brake at one time or another, but, when they saw the extra problems it made in poor braking, plus the strain on the entire drive line, they quickly converted to the safer system of one brake on each rear wheel.

By having only one brake on the entire drive-line, the braking surface was considerably smaller on the Model "T" Ford than with one brake on each rear wheel. Two things resulted: (1) it took longer to stop the car and (2) the brake lining on the band wore out sooner. It was more difficult to replace the lining on the Model "T" Ford brake band, inside the transmission, than it was to remove both rear wheels on a conventional car of the time and replace the lining on both rear bands.

The Model "T" Ford was equipped with what Ford termed an "emergency brake" which acted on the inside of a very small rear brake drum at each rear wheel when the hand lever was pulled all the way back. There was no lining; the steel brake shoe contacted the inside of the steel brake drum, so the thought of using this to bring the car to a stop in an emergency situation was out. At best, when everything was working properly, that brake would probably hold the car on a level spot if there was no wind blowing.

In actual practice, most Model "T" Ford owners kept a brick to chock the wheel when they parked on any kind of grade. Around the time of World War I, some accessory makers brought out a kit whereby the owner replaced the original Model "T" Ford brake drums with much larger drums furnished in the kit, as well as outside brake bands and all the necessary parts and rods, etc., thus installing considerably better brakes than had been built into the car by Ford. One of these manufacturers referred to his accessory kit as Rocky Mountain brakes.

I have never heard of anyone's making anything to replace the disasterous Model "T" steering arrangement, however. Ford kept this same brake and steering system on all 15 million Model "T" Fords made from 1909 until mid 1927. The roads in this country were such in 1909 that it was difficult to go too fast, so some people will contend that the Model "T" Ford was not any more unsafe than any other car of the times. Obviously, this is not so or there would have been no need for Rocky Mountain type brakes.

Had the Model "T" Ford brakes and steering been redesigned after it became obvious that they were so bad, as did a few other manufacturers who used the drive-line brake for a short time, history might have been kinder to them. Had Ford been a small manufacturer, or had the Model "T" been replaced, or even modernized, it might have been excusable; but every other car on the road was a Model "T" Ford for over ten years and Henry Ford was one of the wealthiest men in this country. His company was one of the most profitable in *ANY* industry.

Henry Ford Loses An Early Law Suit

Just about this time, Henry Ford had to contend with one Frederick W. Ball who had a patent on a certain type of reversing mechanism for a transmission. Mr. Ball took Henry Ford to court for infringing on his patent and won. Part of the settlement was that Ford would pay Mr. Ball one dollar for every car built with this type of transmission. Neither Mr. Ball nor Mr. Ford realized at the time that Ford would build fifteen million Model "T" Fords, at a dollar each to Mr. Ball!

Roy Chapin And Friends From The Hudson Motor Car Co.

The addition of Hugh Chalmers to the sales manager's job at Chalmers-Detroit did not have the desired effect of selling a lot more cars. Soon after this addition to the management, Mr. Chapin and Mr. Coffin left the company. One of their good friends, and a fellow engineer from their previous association with Oldsmobile, had married into the Hudson Department Store family of Detroit and together they agreed to put up the money for the new car. The Hudson first appeared in 1909.

C. Y. Knight's Engine Helps British Firm Win Dewar Trophy

An inventive gentlemen named Charles Y. Knight was responsible for a British automobile company's winning the Dewar Trophy for outstanding development by an automobile manufacturer for 1909, just as Cadillac had done the year before. Mr. Knight, a United States citizen, had developed a "sleeve valve" engine which was extremely quiet for its time. The Daimler Co. of England adopted it exclusively for their cars and continued using it until the start of World War II. Many of the Royal Family cars were supplied by Daimler down through the years.

Mr. Knight had made a car of his own design in Chicago but couldn't really get the company to go over very well. Its best selling point was the engine. He tried to get other people in the United States interested but didn't really get very far. He then went to England and Europe where Daimler and also manufacturers in France and Germany were interested. The quality of gasoline and oil produced by the refining process of the times allowed carbon build-up inside the engine which actually formed a better seal between the pistons and the sleeve valves and the efficiency of the engine improved with use.

The Daimler Co. actually won the Dewar Trophy mainly because of the engine designed by Mr. Knight of Chicago, U.S.A. Eventually, the Knight engine was installed in some cars in the United States; the two most well known were the Willys-Knight of Toledo and the Stearns-Knight of Cleveland.

1910

Kettering's Genius Solves An Early Problem

A man who contributed much to the automobile industry was Charles F. Kettering. Kettering actually got his start in business working for the National Cash Register Co., of Dayton, Ohio. He made many improvements on them, making them electric and also automatic. One of the major problems with the cash register was that a sales clerk in a department store, for example, had no way of keeping a record except what was written down in the sales book. If these sales clerks happened to have "sticky fingers" they would put the money in their own pockets and would not enter the amount in their sales book, so no one knew about the sale. The system Mr. Kettering invented meant that the clerk had to ring up the sale, which made a record of it, before the cash register would open to get the customer's change and receipt. What Mr. Kettering did was to come up with an electric motor which was very small, yet had a lot of power or "torque" which only had to work for an instant, just long enough to ring up the sale and open the drawer.

The automobile and its problems had always fascinated Mr. Kettering, and although he was truly a genius of an inventor, he never aspired to build his own car. Mr. Kettering was to the automobile business what Thomas Edison was to electricity. Mr. Kettering first tackled the problem of automobile ignition. That is what makes the spark plugs fire at just the right time with just the right amount of spark. Until this time, automobile ignition was quite uncertain and it was really one of the drawbacks to happy motoring. Keetering's ignition system was to put precision where there had formerly been uncertainty in design. Quality control was improved in the making of the parts. Cars had been using magneto ignition to make the spark. Magneto ignition is O.K. once the engine is turning over fast enough and if the engine doesn't run too fast. The only way to get the engine to turn over fast enough to start in those days was to crank it.

Mr. Kettering, and his boss at the cash register company, Mr. Deeds, formed their own company while still working full time for the cash register company. They could only work evenings and weekends. The company they formed was the Dayton Experimental Laboratories Company. Eventually it became known just by its initials: DELCO. Mr. Kettering actually worked on the ignition system for over a year before getting all the bugs worked out.

Legend has it that one of the chief engineers from Cadillac in Detroit came to test drive a Cadillac which Mr. Kettering had equipped with the new ignition system. All went well and Mr. Kettering drove the Cadillac engineer back to the railroad depot and saw him onto the train going back to Detroit, but when Mr. Kettering went back to start the demonstrator car, it would not start; a connection had come unsoldered.

The new ignition system became standard equipment on the 1910 Cadillac. By that time Cadillac was just making one model car, the Thirty, so named because it developed 30 horsepower from its four-cylinder engine. Cadillac ordered 150 enclosed bodies, and is generally considered to be the first car maker to offer cars with "ready made" enclosed bodies. Prior to this time, all enclosed cars were specially ordered to the customer's desire.

This same year, 1910, Packard also made a four cylinder car of thirty horsepower which Packard called its Packard Thirty.

The Impulse Buying Of Durant Breaks G.M.

By late 1910, the buying spree of Mr. Durant of General Motors was still in full swing. He had bought entire companies or controlling interest in manufacturers of complete automobiles, as well as companies that supplied parts such as castings, forgings, wheels, axles, etc. The idea of buying up supply companies was not new to Mr. Durant. When active in the carriage business, he had done this with wheels, varnish, axles, and such component parts of carriages. He had also done this with Buick before Ben Briscoe put the bug in his ear about buying up entire automobile manufacturers. Mr. Durant, through Buick, was instrumental in having an axle company, a spark plug company and a body building company move to Flint.

The result of the two-year buying spree was that General Motors was now over extended and deeply in debt. The original car company, Buick, was still showing a good profit; Cadillac was showing a profit also, due mainly to the Leland leadership; Oakland was showing a slight profit. The other companies were just about holding their own or else showing losses. Buick and Cadillac were carrying almost the entire load. Had Mr. Durant carried out his idea of controlling his supply companies in a more conservative manner, and had he put some thought behind some of the money he spent, instead of doing it by whim or impulse, history might have been kinder to him.

One of the most expensive mistakes was the purchase of the Heany Lamp Company. Some of their patents were questionable. Durant knew this but took a chance that everything would be straightened out and G.M. would come out on top. By the time the lawyers were finished in court, the patents were no good. Heany was a worthless purchase at a total of over ten million dollars, which is more than Oldsmobile and Buick combined had cost.

In the summer of 1910, Henry M. Leland took an extended vacation in Europe leaving his son, Wilfred, to keep things running smoothly at Cadillac. While he was away, noting how Europe was preparing for war, things came to a head at General Motors. The expansion had gone too far for good common business sense. The money had run out. Durant toured the Western states trying to get banks to put up some money, but none would. G.M. already owed over 200 banks throughout the country through lines of credit. Buick owed about seven million.

General Motors was broke!

One stock holder came to Durant and told him of a Boston bank which might be convinced to help. The one bank could not swing it all alone so several others were called in —over twenty in all. The bankers had already decided to keep Buick only and to close down the rest of General Motors. But two people had not been counted on, Wilfred Leland of Cadillac and Ralph van Vetchen, a banker from Chicago. All of the group were gathered for one September day in 1910, then into the evening and eventually into the early hours of the next morning. Wilfred Leland was constantly reminding the bankers of the reputation and quality of Cadillac and how it would become even more profitable, if allowed to continue. This was out of character for Wilfred who usually let his famous father do this sort of thing. But his father was in Europe and so Wilfred took the bull by the horns and got the job done. It is said that Ralph van Vetchen was the first banker to agree with Wilfred Leland that the entire General Motors was worth saving, not just Buick.

Two years earlier it had been this same Ralph van Vetchen who took a chance and loaned railroad man Walter P. Chrysler the $4,300.00 to buy that Locomobile touring car from the 1908 automobile show.

The final result was that General Motors would receive 12.5 million by agreeing to the following conditions: (1) pay back 20 million in five years. . . (2) put some of the bankers on the General Motors Board of Directors. . . (3) allow Durant *NO* control, but however remain on the G.M. Board of Directors. Either Durant would agree to those conditions or all would go down the tube and be lost. Faced with no other alternative, Durant agreed to the terms. At Durant's suggestion, Charles W. Nash was made general manager of Buick; he had been its production manager and, prior to that, he had been third in command at the carriage company, behind only Durant and Dort, the founding partners.

Mr. Durant And Mr. Ford Compared

Henry Ford and William C. Durant were as different as any two men could be in some ways, yet very much alike in other respects. Both married girls whose first names were Clara; the Fords remained married but the Durant's were divorced in 1908 and each re-married someone else. Both ruled their companies with an iron hand, allowing no one else to make decisions for them and usually consulting no one else about their decisions. Both were extremely impulsive, but Ford was extremely stubborn in addition — two qualities which did not make him well liked or easy to get along with. Durant would listen to new ideas on anything; Ford would only listen to new ideas concerning his favorite subject, the Model "T".

Ford wanted nothing to do with bankers if he could help it. He was a farm boy and didn't grasp accounting all that well; he would rather hire someone to take care of that end of the business. Durant accepted bankers because they could make available the large sums of money he needed to put together his grand ideas. He knew that they were entitled to a fair

82

Source: *National Auto History Collection
of the Detroit Public Library*

Louis Chevrolet Driving A Race Car

Source: *National Auto History Collection of the Detroit Public Library*

Louis Chevrolet Driving A Race Car

Source: *National Auto History Collection
of the Detroit Public Library*

Louis Chevrolet Driving A Race Car

(Caption)

Louis Chevrolet Driving A Race Car (3 different)

Louis Chevrolet is in what could be the same car painted with three different numbers for different occasions. In #10 he is shown with the familiar cigarette; this photo was posed prior to a race since faces and hands are clean. In #31, the grueling race shows in the dirt and expressions of both Louis Chevrolet and his riding mechanic. This was in the era when Louis Chevrolet and Bob Burman were the chief drivers for the Buick factory-sponsored racing team. Louis' brothers, Gaston and Arthur, were also in auto racing. All three brothers had raced in the Indianapolis Memorial Day 500 mile race at various times. Gaston remained in racing, but never achieved the fame of Louis, although Gaston won an Indianapolis 500. Arthur was too conservative a driver to win enough races, and eventually ceased driving race cars.

return on their investment. He understood the stock market and, before he became interested in Buick in 1904, he would often spend months at a time in New York City at Wall Street playing the stock market. Durant was a millionaire by age forty; Ford was relatively unknown at age forty.

When Ford wanted some plan carried out, he would delegate someone to get it done; quite often this delegate was James Couzens who was a bear for work. Durant, however, would have to locate someone who was a specialist in the particular field involved, then delegate that man to carry out his ideas.

Their personalities were, indeed, quite different. Mr. Durant was said to be quite charming and a super salesman and quite un-predictable as to what his next whim might be. Mr. Ford, history shows us, was just as un-predictable as Durant but without the charm and salesmanship of Durant. Ford was quite domineering and stubborn; he thrived on the power he had over someone's career and enjoyed employees' being in constant fear of him that he might get rid of them without reason or provocation.

Ford managed to get rid of all those who knew him when he was poor and still struggling and needed them. C. H. Wills, James Couzens, John and Horace Dodge are excellent examples. Durant, on the other hand, did not hold grudges and deliberately try to ruin the career of someone who happened to rub him the wrong way, as Henry Ford was constantly doing after he became wealthy and could buy anyone he wanted.

Henry Ford's salary was raised to $75,000.00 a year in 1910 it had been $3,000.00 a year in 1903.

The Dodge Brothers Make Long Range Plans

The Dodge brothers learned, early in their years of dealing with Henry Ford, that no one was about to change his mind. The Dodge brothers had found better ways of building parts of the various models of Ford cars since 1903, which would have been improvements, but Ford flatly refused to consider such new ideas if anything either cost more or took longer. The fact that a better quality car would result was of no importance to Henry Ford. The Dodge's wanted to let the Model "T" evolve and improve but Henry Ford said "NO".

By 1910 the Dodge's, who still owned 10% of the Ford Motor Co., were considering the idea of making a car of their own to be of extremely good quality, yet not to be terribly high-priced. They had built parts for Olds and now had several years experience in building cheap parts for Ford; so they knew what to avoid. Now, the Dodge's wanted to build a good quality car. Although no definite time had been set for the project, in 1910 they bought a large tract of land in the nearby city of Hamtramck, where they built a bigger and more modern plant, as it was needed anyway to build the parts for Ford.

1911

Henry Ford Finds A Way To Keep His Name In The News Free

An event took place this year which also shows how stubborn and arrogant and attention-demanding was Henry Ford. The event was his "winning" of the Selden Patent

William Howard Taft and Charles Evans Hughes in a White Steamer

Passengers in this White steamer touring car include William Howard Taft and Charles Evans Hughes. It is not certain whether Taft was still President when this photo was taken. This is not a White House car.

Many White steamers were painted white.

Despite its success in the steam car field, 1910 was the last year the White was steam-powered. The following year they switched to gasoline engines. The White Sewing Machine Co. was the parent company.

suit; it was no victory because the patent was due to exprire in 1912 anyway. Ford spent money on lawyers in this suit to keep his name before the public and to get front page newspaper space as a champion of the little man fighting the bad guys. Actually, Henry Ford, himself, was wealthier and had made more money than any of those involved in the Selden Patent.

Back in 1876, when the Centennial Exposition had been held in Philadelphia, patent attorney George Selden was fascinated by the two-cycle gasoline engine displayed by George Brayton. Selden mulled things over in his mind and made sketches. In 1879, he APPLIED for a patent on his idea of a self-propelled vehicle. It was to be run on liquid fuel (gasoline is a liquid fuel), have a clutch so that the engine could run while the vehicle was standing still, and have a method of steering the vehicle, along with other features. In order to keep the patent PENDING, Selden kept filling various revisions to keep it alive and pending for 16 years as the law permitted in those days. When it was due to run out, he applied for and was granted a patent in 1895, which meant that it was to run until 1912.

Selden, himself, could do little with the patent, so he sold it in 1899 for $10,000.00 to a group of promotors of *ELECTRIC* vehicles. The promoters had hopes of keeping all gasoline-powered cars off the road by refusing to let them be built until 1912 when electric cars would be completely refined, the promoters hoped. Things didn't work out that way and soon the Columbia gasoline car was being built by the Electric Vehicle Co. and very few electrically powered cars were being built. The promoters did a bit of legal maneuvering and got the gasoline car makers to pay them a little royalty rather than go to court, which the makers of the various gasoline-powered cars could not afford to do at that time in case they lost their cases.

In 1903, Henry Ford either never applied for or else applied and was refused a license, but in any case, Ford didn't pay the royalties. The bluff was called. At this time the owners of the patent were still making some money and could afford lawyer's fees and court costs. The case dragged on until 1911. Meanwhile, in 1909, the Electric Vehicle Co. folded and was re-organized as Columbia, but it was gone a couple of years later.

All this time Ford advertised that the Ford Motor Co. would post a bond for anyone who wanted one, so that potential customers would not be afraid to buy a Ford due to the legal battle. Only about fifty buyers of the 75,000 or so cars Ford built from 1903 to 1911 took the Ford Motor Co. up on it.

The final court decision was that the patent was valid, but that neither Ford, nor anyone else, had violated it, chiefly because the patent covered a vehicle with a two-cycle engine and all Fords, and most other cars of the time, were then using the more practical four-cycle engine.

Arthur Chevrolet Breaks Down At "Indy"

Arthur Chevrolet drove a racer in the first Indianapolis 500 mile Memorial Day race. His car broke down after about 75 miles and was through for the day.

Walter Chrysler Joins Buick And General Motors

By now Walter P. Chrysler was in charge of the shops of the American Locomotive Co. in Pittsburgh and he had just paid off the loan on the Locomobile touring car which he had bought at the Chicago Automobile Show in 1908. It just so happened that a director of the American Locomotive Co. was also a director of General Motors. He knew of Mr. Chrysler's good work at Pittsburgh. He got Mr. Chrysler and Mr. Nash together and the result was that

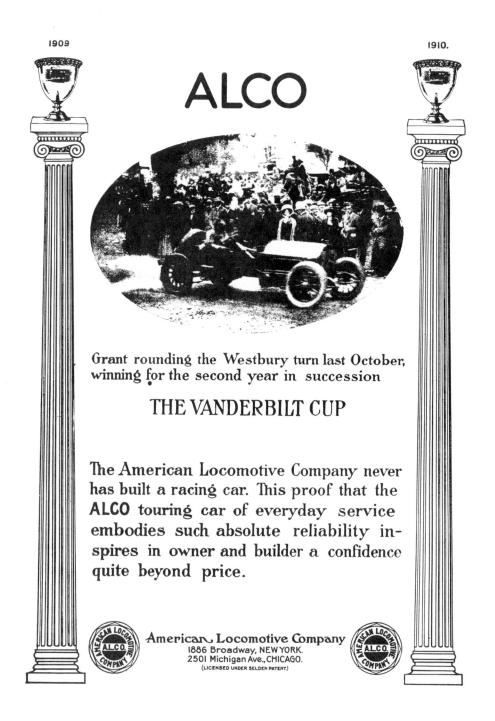

1909.   1910.

ALCO

Grant rounding the Westbury turn last October,
winning for the second year in succession

THE VANDERBILT CUP

The American Locomotive Company never
has built a racing car. This proof that the
ALCO touring car of everyday service
embodies such absolute reliability in-
spires in owner and builder a confidence
quite beyond price.

American Locomotive Company
1886 Broadway, NEW YORK.
2501 Michigan Ave., CHICAGO.
(LICENSED UNDER SELDEN PATENT.)

Walter P. Chrysler was an employee of the American Locomotive Co. during 1910 when
this ad appeared, but he had nothing to do with the ALCO automobile. He was in the
Pittsburgh repair shops.

Chrysler became in charge of Buick production, which had been Mr. Nash's old job before his promotion to the general manager of Buick. Ironically, this same American Locomotive Co. which Mr. Chrysler worked for, was just winding down its production of its own car using their initials ALCO. Mr. Chrysler had nothing to do with the ALCO automobile. It was a big, heavy car, but sales volume was not enough`to make it a money-making enterprise, so they concentrated on just making railroad locomotives after five or six years of making a relatively few cars.

Durant Forms The Chevrolet Motor Co.

After Mr. Durant's removal from General Motors' control, he decided to get something going again. Mr. Louis Chevrolet had left Buick when the company gave up racing to cut down expenses. By now, those bankers in charge of General Motors were too conservative to put money into something as flamboyant as automobile racing. It was beneath their dignity. Louis Chevrolet knew enough about automobiles to be a reasonably good designer.

Durant realized that General Motors was not going to build a low priced car, and he saw the success Ford was having with the Model "T". He remembered the success of the Buick Model 10, a low-priced car which the new heads of General Motors decided to stop making because it was low-priced and they didn't want to be associated with a cheap car. Durant hired Louis Chevrolet to start work on designing a low-priced car. He also contacted some of his friends and former associates in Flint.

By the end of 1911, the Chevrolet Motor Co. was formally organized. A few experimental cars had been made but the price would have been over $2,000.00 — not the low price Durant had wanted. When the Chevrolet Motor Co. came into existence, Louis Chevrolet was the designer of the car. He worked for the company which had his name but had no money invested in it and was not even on the board of directors. Of the three Chevrolet brothers, only Louis had a job of any importance with the Chevrolet Motor Co.; Arthur and Gaston remained with automobile racing.

Front Doors Begin Appearing On New Cars

It was about this time that front doors began appearing on new U.S. built cars. Several manufacturers made them accessories. Some even made them available for their past model cars already in the hands of owners. They were originally called "fore" doors for foreward, as on a ship, to distinguish them from rear doors.

Adding front doors was another step away from horse and wagon days, when sometimes teamsters would have to stand up to guide the horses and needed plenty of room to work the reins. Teamsters also used the spoke or hub of the wagon wheel to step up directly to the seat and reins. By 1911 enough automobiles were in the hands of the general public for them to insist on such an elementary comfort as front doors, just as they did a few years earlier with the elimination of the rear entrance design, replacing it with the much more practiced side (rear) doors.

1912

The Starter Is Here To Stay

The electrical genius of Charles Kettering came to light again. He attacked the problem of starting the engine by a method other than the hand crank. The starter became standard equipment on the 1912 Cadillac which still had a four-cylinder engine, still had the steering on the right, and was still their "Model Thirty." The Cadillac people, under Henry Leland, had tried to make a starter system but they really never got the right combination together, mainly because what they had was too big and bulky among a few other drawbacks.

What Kettering did was to combine the three major electrical components of the car which were starting, lighting, and ignition, into one dependable setup. His first system on the 1912 Cadillac was crude, but it DID work. It used 24 volts to start the engine and six volts to run the car and had a combination starter-generator to generate 24 volts while only putting in six. It was crude, but it was so much better than cranking.

A couple of years later he improved it, due largely to the invention of the over-running clutch by Vincent Bendix. The Bendix over-running clutch is still used on starters today. Within three years of its introduction, or by 1915, 97% of the car manufacturers in the United States had some sort of a starting system available, whether standard equipment or at extra cost. Ford was one of those who did NOT offer a starter of any kind for the Model "T" until several years later.

Several starter systems of the various car builders of the time used the DELCO system. Over in France, any starting system was known as Le Delco whether it was made by DELCO or by a competitor, just as today we have several brands of facial tissue, but they are all called Kleenex; gelatin deserts are called Jell-O and the list could go on.

For their self-starting system, Cadillac was again awarded the Dewar Trophy for the most distinguished achievement of 1912. It was the same honor which had been bestowed on Cadillac in 1908 and the only time a car maker outside England was to receive the honor twice. This was the same honor Charles Y. Knight was responsible for in 1909 due to his sleeve-valve-engine design for the Daimler Company of England.

Studebaker Absorbs E.M.F. To Save Face

The E.M.F.-Studebaker combine had not worked out too well although it had survived a little longer than the two year (1908-1910) span of General Motors under the original control of William C. Durant. Studebaker had been in business sixty years in 1912 and had a fine reputation for horse-drawn vehicles. Studebaker had only designed one car, and that was an electric model which was now almost completely phased out. All the gasoline-powered cars from Studebaker were someone's else's design, with Studebaker providing the bodies and the assembly facilities. To keep their good reputation in the family transportation field, they bought out the other parties involved in the E.M.F.-Studebaker Corp. in 1912. They did a lot of model shuffling and then changed the cars formerly named E.M.F. to Studebaker. They were mostly in the medium price range, such as Buick and Oldsmobile, etc.

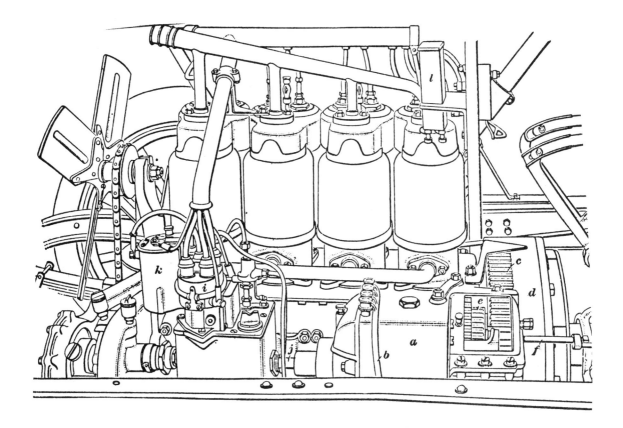

1912 Cadillac Cutaway Drawing

Self starter units are shown in "A", "B", "C", "D", "E", in the drawing. "I" and "K" show the ignition system units which Cadillac had been using since 1910. Cylinders cast individually was a common practice in this era. Cylinders cast in pairs were also used by many engine makers. The fan belt was made in many individual sections riveted together. The fan belt only drove the fan.

94

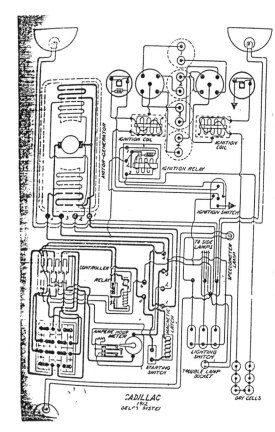

CADILLAC

MODEL 40 (1912). SERIAL NOS. 61,006 TO 75,000
DELCO GENERATING, STARTING AND LIGHTING SYSTEM
DELCO IGNITION

BATTERY.—Battery is 24 volt, 45 ampere-hour. Battery is divided into four groups of three cells each. The controller connects the four groups in series for starting and in parallel for charging. Six dry cells connected in series supply current for the auxiliary ignition. The two-wire system is used.

IGNITION.—There are two distinct ignition systems, employing two sets of spark plugs. Breaker contacts separate .010 inch. When the contacts are closed, the contact blade and clip separate .015 inch.

OILING.—Put 3 or 4 drops of light engine oil in each of the timer bearing oilers every two weeks. If the car is driven more than 500 miles in two weeks, the oiling must be done every 500 miles.

TIMING.—Breaker contacts begin to separate when the flywheel marking "1 & 4 D. C." is ½ inch past the indicator, spark control lever and breaker assembly in the fully retarded position.

FIRING ORDER.—The firing order is 1, 2, 4, 3.

SPARK PLUG GAPS.—Spark plug gaps are .020 to .025 inch.

STARTER-GENERATOR.—Model No. 1. Starter and generator are combined into one unit. Starter is connected to the engine through a sliding pinion, meshed with the flywheel gear by the operator. Running freely, starter takes 14 amperes, armature revolving at 1800 R.P.M.

GENERATOR.—Generator current regulation is by reverse series field.

Amperes	Generator Data	R.P.M.
Neutral		300
5		500
12		1000
17-22		1500

Operating freely as a motor with the overrunning clutch at the driving end as the only retarding force, generator takes 4.5 amperes. Charging rate is varied by changing the value of the shunt resistance, located between the two top terminals on the "Charge" side of the controller switch. Two shunts are available, a single strand which permits a low charging rate, and a double strand which permits a high charging rate.

RELAY.—Relay is mounted above the controller switch. Relay closes at 7-9 miles per hour or 300-350 R.P.M. of the armature, and opens at 5-7 miles per hour or 250-300 R.P.M. of the armature. Charging current is 1-3 amperes at closing, and the discharge current is 0-1 ampere at the opening of relay contacts.

1912 Cadillac Wiring Diagram And Description

Wiring Diagram of 1912 Cadillac electrical system, including the starter system with 24 volt battery.

Although the coil and breaker point ignition system was introduced on the 1910 Model 30, Cadillac retained the magneto arrangement as an emergency or backup system through the 1912 models.

By 1913, they were confident enough to drop the magneto system and depend completely on the coil and breaker points.

Also in 1913, the system was improved so that only one six-volt battery was necessary, not 24 volts as on the 1912 models.

Source: *National Auto History Collection
of the Detroit Public Library*

1912 Buick

Source: *National Auto History Collection
of the Detroit Public Library*

The 1912 Cadillac and 1912 Buick

While still separate parts of General Motors, the large Buick had a definite resemblance to the Cadillac. Both cars had four-cylinder engines.

The rods at the center of the windshield were braces, the other end being attached to the front of the car's frame. The others are leather straps connecting the front of the top to the car's frame. The windshield did not support the top. The top half of the windshield could be folded down for added ventilation as shown in the Cadillac photo. A couple of years later, when metal cowls became standard equipment, the windshield became more rigid and was able to support the front half of the top without braces or straps.

Walter Chrysler And Charles Nash Promoted By G.M.

In November, Charles W. Nash was elevated from President of Buick to President of General Motors; Walter P. Chrysler was elevated from General Manager of Buick to President of Buick, the position just vacated by Nash.

Bankers Influence In The Auto Industry

Since bankers were now in control of General Motors, as well as of the floundering United States Motors, and because of the considerable amounts of money needed in both operations, a bit of explanation of how this had affected the automobile business, and also our culture in the United States, is now in order.

One of the chief reasons General Motors failed in 1910 was that Durant could not find bankers to put up money for his grand ideas. To Durant, his ideas seemed perfectly logical, but to no one else — or at least to no one else with a lot of money. Then came the more than twenty bankers who were gathered together by the Boston group. They took the chance. By 1912 it was obvious that the gamble was a smart one. Something was happening that they did not realize would happen; the public wanted to buy their own automobiles and attain the independence that car ownership brought. This told the bankers that the automobile was here to stay. What the bankers did in 1912 and in the succeeding years was the foundation for changing the way the people in the United States, and eventually the world, lived.

A banker in Frankfurt, Germany, is generally credited with being the one responsible for devloping the idea of really high financing. His name was Meyer A. Rothschild. He had five sons and had four of them move to different large cities in Europe to help finance kings and countries. All during the 1800's they had done this and became very wealthy in the process. Often they would be financing both sides of the same war — the outcome being decided by which king borrowed the most money.

The way a king obtained more money than his enemy did was to make more concessions to those in control of the money, the Rothschilds. All wars usually ended in a balance of power where everyone was rather well matched militarily. The way a king had of getting Rothschild money was to appoint people that the Rothschild group named to high ranking positions in his particular government. The Rothschild employee was then able to see that the interest on the loan, which the king had made to go to war, was being paid back, along with the original loan. When the loan was almost paid off, things were stirred up again making another loan necessary to get ready for another conflict. The Rothschilds established "central banks" in capitals all over Europe and used this method of controlling his money to keep a particular king in line.

Until the last of the 1800's, the United States was primarily an agricultural country. The advent of the railroad and the telegraph helped considerably to knit our country together. The Baltimore and Ohio was the first railroad to be chartered to carry goods and passengers. It was controlled by the Kuhn-Loeb & Co. who also controlled the Pennsylvania Railroad. John D. Rockefeller Sr. had to use those railroads to ship his oil to the east and northeast. Both concerns became quite wealthy in the process.

The Rothschilds knew that eventually the large and under-developed Unied States would soon be ripe for high financing. The man in charge here was J. Pierpont Morgan. A partner in the Rothschild firm in Frankfurt had been Jacob Schiff. In 1902, a Schiff daughter, and her husband Felix Warburg and Felix's brother, Paul, moved to the United States from Germany. Paul Warburg married into the Kuhn family of Kuhn-Loeb & Co. Keep in mind that "arranged marriages" were not unusual in European families for financial reasons.

There had been no central bank in the United States since 1836 when it was abolished by President Andrew Jackson.

William Howard Taft was expected to run again for President in 1912; he had been picked in 1908 by Theodore Roosevelt as his successor. However, a difference of opinion between the two developed and Roosevelt decided to run again, himself. Since both were Republicans, this split the Republican Party, and Roosevelt actually ran as a third party candidate against both Republican Taft and Democrat, Woodrow Wilson.

The bankers had no love for Taft because it was during his administration in 1910 that the big bankers' first attempt to get a central bank established, legally, was defeated by the U.S. Congress, largely because President Taft opposed it. However, the proposed constitutional amendment to allow the federal government to collect a graduated income tax was initiated during the Taft administration in 1909. The big bankers put their money behind Wilson and Roosevelt. Both candidates attempted to show how the big money people of Wall Street should be broken up. U.S. Steel of Andrew Carnegie and Standard Oil of John D. Rockefeller were the targets.

It is of interest that Edward M. House wrote a book in 1912 *Philip Dru, Administrator*. In it, he advocated a graduated income tax and a central bank. These are also two of Karl Marx's ten ideas in his *Communist Manifesto*.

When Woodrow Wilson was elected, the national debt was approximately one billion dollars. The average automobile worker was earning about $2.45 a day.

Dr. Diesel's Personal Tragedy

Dr. Rudolph Diesel of Germany invented a spin off of the four-cycle OTTO-type engine except that Dr. Diesel's ran on a somewhat different fuel than gasoline, and it injected the fuel directly into the cylinder instead of using a carburetor or intake manifold system. His engine ran much hotter, so hot in fact that it did not need spark plugs. This was mostly theory, however, as Dr. Diesel had an awful time getting everything to work right.

He had tried in Europe to get his engine produced, but it just had too many complicated drawbacks to be practical for an automobile or for anything else. He decided to come to this country to see what he could do, but he never made it. He sailed from Germany on the Lusitania and, somewhere on the way, he went overboard and was lost at sea. Some say his body washed up on the English side of the Channel. All he left behind in his personal life were a lot of debts and not nearly enough money or insurance to cover them.

1913

Ford Adopts The Assembly Line To Auto Making

Ford refined the idea of assembly line production to the point where this was the year and Ford was the company generally given credit for it. Assembly line production had been used by Olds in the late 1890's, but it was more of a co-ordination of the arrival of raw materials with the scheduling of what to do when, than anything else.

Assembly line production had also been used previously by a supplier of pulley blocks to the British Navy in the French and English War 100 years before. When the war ended, there was no more need for a large quantity of pulleys and the idea was not pursued by any other

Model "T" Fords at the End of the Chassis Assembly Line

Photo shows cars when they were being started for the first time. They were maneuvered into position where the rear wheels were resting in the rollers built into the floor. A hose was connected to the back of the muffler to take fumes outside, then the rollers were turned on to make the car's rear wheels revolve. The driver then took his place on top of the gas tank, switched on the magneto, set the carburetor controls (within easy reach of the driver), then pushed the left pedal all the way down. That engaged the transmission in low gear which, with the rear wheels revolving, made the engine turn over. If everything was put together properly the engine would start. The chassis could then be driven under its own power to get the body, fenders, lights, etc. installed to make a complete automobile.

This method of starting was used for two reasons: first, a new engine is "stiff" and, since Fords did not have starters during this era, they were very hard to crank until broken in for a few minutes at least; second, if the car would not start for some reason, repairs could be made much easier if the body and fenders, etc. were not in the way.

industry at that time. The Model "T" Ford used sixteen magnets shaped like horse shoes that were bolted to the flywheel as part of the system to generate electricity for the ignition system. The assembling of this unit on a moving conveyor belt is what is referred to as the "start" of assembly line production. The system worked well enough to prompt Ford to start assembling other units and also the complete chassis. Men pulled the chassis along with a rope at first and parts were added as they went along. When this idea proved feasible, more permanent methods were installed so that by the end of 1913, assembly line production at Ford was under way on a permanent and expanding basis, and other auto makers were taking note.

Ford also cheapened the Model "T" in 1913, making many of the parts out of steel or iron which formerly had been brass or bass trim. One of the reasons for this cost cutting was that Henry Ford suspected that the Dodge brothers would soon be striking out on their own and he would have to build the engines and other parts in the Ford plants which the Dodge's had been building for Ford for several years. He laid the ground work for starting another new factory.

The new Model "T" Ford also had a dummy left front door. This meant that the driver had to get into the car first by the right door, and then let wife and baby manage the best way they could, or leg it over the dummy driver's door. It was actually only half a door, as we know it today, as Fords in those days were open cars which meant that they had no windows. Which ever method of entry was used came only after the driver had already cranked the engine to get it started, as Fords did not have any way of starting the engine other than the "armstrong starter" method.

James Couzens, business manager at Ford, was also on the City of Detroit's Street Railway Commission by now. When a strike of Street Railway workers was threatened, Couzens retorted by counter threatening to put a thousand Fords on the streets to transport people free. Whether Couzens would have done it or not will never be known, as his calling the bluff of the proposed strikers was enough to stop the strike before it actually materialized.

U.S. Motors Folds and Maxwell Emerges

Of the three combines of General Motors, E.M.F.-Studebaker, and United States Motors, the last to go broke was the U.S. Motors group. U.S. Motors was too deeply in debt to be rescued as a whole, so the bankers actually accomplished at U.S. what they almost accomplished at General Motors in 1910. They kept going the one successful company, re-modeled it, and hoped that the result would eventually be a profitable investment. The only company worth keeping was Maxwell.

Ben Briscoe, of U.S. Motors, had originally put the bug in William Durant's ear about forming the holding company which was General Motors. Briscoe's U.S. Motors had gone under and Briscoe was invited out. Like Durant of General Motors, Briscoe relinquished control of U.S. Motors gracefully, but was not to remain on the new company's board of directors as Durant had been allowed at General Motors. Also, like Durant, he found other backers and began making another car, the Briscoe.

The new Maxwell Motor Co. formed from the remains of U.S. Motors, was headed by Walter Flanders. Almost immediately, the six-cylinder Maxwell appeared from the Everitt car which had been assembled by the Metzger Motor Car Company, controlled by William Metzger, who, ten years earlier, had been the first sales manager for the then new Cadillac Motor Company. This same combine of Everitt, Metzger, and Flanders were the "E", the "M", and the "F" in the E.M.F.-Studebaker Corp. Maxwell also continued to be made as a four-cylinder car.

Louis Chevrolet Leaves The Chevrolet Motor Co.

Durant had continued to manipulate and had managed to lock up the Chevrolet name, which he liked, and to get rid of Louis Chevrolet whom he didn't like. The outward reason for the departure of Mr. Chevrolet was that he wanted the car with his name to be a big, heavy, impressive car and Durant wanted a small, light, and definitely low-priced car. Since Louis Chevrolet was only an employee of Durant and Durant controlled the money, Durant got his way. Louis Chevrolet was a rough-mannered and high-tempered individual and this proved to be the final clash between the two.

Back in 1904, one of the things that helped convince Durant to take over Buick had been the name. It was somewhat unusual, pleasant-sounding, and easy to pronounce. David Buick's and Louis Chevrolet's personalities were almost exactly opposite, Buick being more quiet and plodding, and Chevrolet being hot-tempered and impulsive. It is not certain whether Buick and Chevrolet ever knew each other, as Buick left Durant's employ just about the time Chevrolet started as a race car driver at the Buick Motor Co. Neither had been born in this country; David Buick was born in Scotland, Louis Chevrolet was born in Switzerland.

Also, in 1913, Durant managed to interest other bankers in lending him two and three quarter million to get Chevrolet's production of a low-priced car under way.

Graduated Tax Becomes Law Despite The Constitution

After the inauguration of Woodrow Wilson as President of the United States, the necessary majority of the states ratified the constitutional amendment setting up a graduated income tax. This amendment was sold because most people didn't make enough money to pay the tax and the poor and the middle class looked on it as a way the rich would pay more. What the average individual had not done was to read the proposed amendment and see the loop holes built into it. For instance, charitable contributions and interest payments were deductible. Since the super rich actually wanted the income tax amendment passed, they had set up tax free trusts or foundations whereby they could legally get by with paying very little in taxes, yet no one else could control their trusts or foundations except people whom they designated. By the time the amendment was ratified in 1913, the super rich trusts and foundations were already set up and in operation. Also, in 1913, the Federal Reserve Bill was passed. This took control of the money supply *OUT* of the U. S. Government's hands, as provided by the Constitution, and put it into a private corporation's hands.

The Federal Reserve Bill was passed in December, 1913 as the Senate was anxious to go home for Christmas recess. At once, Congressman Charles A. Lindbergh, Sr., whose aviator son would become a hero 14 years later, strongly denounced it. Even today, 1913 is the year mentioned by many financiers as the down-turning point for the United States economy.

1914

Ford Pulls The Biggest Publicity Stunt Of All Time!

In the first week of January, the Ford Motor Co. announced the best publicity stunt any company has ever come out with, before or since. It said that it would pay all of its workers at least $5.00 a day. There were provisions that the worker must be employed a certain length of time (6 months) and also that he must be doing his job properly. This made Henry Ford a hero again in the eyes of the car-buying public, as did the winning of the Selden Patent case in 1911, and he was now considered champion of the people looking out for the ordinary working man. By Henry Ford's own admission, the idea was only partly his. James Couzens was equally responsible for it. The company, however, was controlled by Henry Ford and his name was on the cars the company built, so he was given credit by the ordinary citizen.

The amount of $5.00 a day was arrived at completely as a publicity stunt. Henry Ford and James Couzens realized that they were going to have to do something soon to quell the idea that Henry Ford was growing extremely wealthy at the expense of the workers at the Ford Motor Co. The company had made $25 million profit for the year between August 1, 1912, and July 31, 1913, and was on its way on topping that figure. Ford Motor Co. did, in fact, top that figure for the following year, making $30 million profit, despite doubling the worker's pay for the last half of that period. Ford Motor Co. paid $2 million in dividends a month for several months, during that period. During this same period a 500% dividend to the stockholders was declared more than once. Mr. Ford himself, owned between 55% and 60% of the Ford Motor Co. stock by this time.

In the summer of 1914, Ford announced the first of what we know today as a factory rebate. If the Ford Motor Co. sold over 300,000 new cars from August 1, 1914, to August 1, 1915, the company would send a refund check of $50.00 to each buyer. The company sold the cars, so the refund checks were sent out. Also, in the summer of 1914, Ford announced a big expansion program to begin at the River Rouge plant in Dearborn.

In the summer of 1914, the two Dodge brothers incorporated their own company to build cars. By now, the Dodge brothers had resigned as Ford Motor Co. directors and had ceased making parts for Ford, but still retained their 10% of the Ford Motor Co. stock which they had acquired in 1903.

This was the first year when a Model "T" Ford could be purchased only in black. Prior to this, other colors had been available. For another five years it was possible to get a new Ford with dark blue instead of black wheels if one so desired.

It should be noted that the graduated income tax and Federal Reserve System took effect on the working people of the country at approximately the same time that the wages of the Ford Motor Co. were doubled.

Dodge's Form Their Own Company To Make Complete Cars

The date on which the Dodge Brothers Company was officially incorporated was July 17, 1914. Within six months, over 20,000 people applied to become Dodge Brothers' dealers. Production began in mid-November and the company managed to assemble a couple of hundred cars by the end of the year. These cars were referred to as 1915 models and will be described in the next chapter.

Walter Chrysler Modernizes The Cars From Buick

As general manager of Buick, Walter P. Chrysler could see that the time for modernization of the car had come. For the 1914 models, Buick made three major changes: (1) The controls were switched to the other side so that the driver now sat on the left on all Buick cars. (2) The DELCO starting, lighting, and ignition system was adopted for all Buick cars. (3) The most expensive Buick cars were made with a six-cylinder engine. The decision to hold off on the six-cylinder engine until after the installation of a dependable starter system was indeed wise. A six-cylinder engine is very hard to crank. Buick continued to build four-cylinder cars, too.

Durant Gets Financing For Chevrolet Production

In order to get Chevrolet production going on a larger scale, Durant borrowed two and three quarter million dollars from a group of banks. Durant used this money to considerably expand and develop new facilities for production of Chevrolet's operations. Durant calculated he could sell 25,000 cars, but he was only able to produce 5,000 cars. Durant was also vice president of the Monroe company. Monroe built a small car but had no dealers as such, so, that until Chevrolet got into high production a year or two later, Chevrolet dealers also sold the Monroe car. Its price was a little cheaper than Chevrolet but it was not nearly as powerful as Chevrolet.

Cadillac Has A Patent Problem

Cadillac was going through one of its "in-between" years. They had not significantly changed the car since their self-starter was introduced for the 1912 models. The Cadillac still had right hand drive and the engine and transmission were still the same basic units as when the Model Thirty was first introduced in 1909, although they had evolved and were constantly improved through the years. Cadillac brought out a two-speed axle for the 1914 Model Thirty but someone else already had a patent on a two-speed rear axle almost identical to it. A law suit followed and Cadillac had to pay damages plus had to stop making its two-speed rear axle. All this resulted in Cadillac's selling less than half the number of cars in 1914 which they had sold in 1913.

Maxwell Hires A Famous Racing Driver

The winner of the first Indianapolis 500 Race which had been held in 1911 was Ray Harroun. He went to work for the newly re-organized Maxwell Company in 1914 as chief engineer. Maxwell had dropped its six-cylinder models and was now concentrating on a low-priced car with a four-cylinder engine. Its price range was a little above Ford's or about the same as the Chevrolet 490, but not quite as high as the four-cylinder Buick's price.

The Austrian Archduke Is Shot In An Automobile

The war, for which Europe had been preparing for several years, began. The fact that the Austrian Archduke was riding in an automobile when he was shot and killed is merely incidental. As early as 1910, Henry Leland of Cadillac took a vacation trip to Europe and had noticed how the Europeans, especially the Germans, were preparing for war.

Bankers Control Several Major Auto Firms

Chevrolet, Maxwell, and the General Motors group of Buick, Cadillac, Oldsmobile, Oakland, etc., were now all under control of bankers in 1914, which represented about 68,000 cars built for that year.

The "Quad" Truck Has Many New Innovations

The Jeffery Co. of Kenosha, Wisconsin, came out with a truck model which they called the "QUAD". That word "QUAD" has its roots in the Latin word "FOUR". It was a big truck and had four-wheel driving power, four-wheel brakes, and four-wheel steering, as well as a four-cylinder engine. During World War I, the French and British armies ordered several thousand QUADS. One of the reasons for QUAD success was the new clutch system that was used called Borg and Beck, named after its inventors.

The purpose of any clutch is to allow the engine to run while the vehicle itself remains standing still. When the clutch is engaged, the engine's power is connected by friction plates, strong springs, and a system of levers to the transmission which leads to making the wheels revolve. The clutch also assists in shifting gears.

Until now, all clutches had been either leather-faced-cone-type, or a multiple disc type, or a type with cork lining. Some ran in oil and some were "dry", depending on the type of material used by the particular clutch manufacturer. The leather-faced-cone-type clutch engaged smoothly, but was prone to slip; the multiple disc-type was quite strong and not prone to slip, but did not engage nearly as smoothly as the cone-type clutch. The cork type was extremely smooth and positive-acting, but would not take any slippage. The Borg and Beck clutch, however, had the smooth positive action of the cork type and had the strength of the multiple disc type. Since the Borg and Beck clutch performed so well on the QUAD truck and was cheaper to build and maintain, other manufacturers of cars as well as trucks gradually switched to the Borg and Beck type over the years.

This is the first year when the name of its cars and trucks was changed to "Jeffery" and the name "Rambler" dropped.

A DuPont Executive Buys Some General Motors Stock

The E. I. DuPont de Nemours Co. of Wilmington, Delaware, was making a lot of money-selling munitions. Their treasurer was John Jacob Rascob; he bought 500 shares of General Motors stock in 1914. The president of the company, Pierre S. DuPont, then bought 2,000 shares of General Motors stock.

The Good Roads Project Hits A Snag

Roy Chapin of Hudson still remembered the Detroit to New York trip he made in 1901 in that curved-dash Oldsmobile over those horrible roads. He made it a personal project to devote all the time and money he could to improving the road system of this country. In 1914, he became head of a group of automobile executives who pledged money to help. Then the project hit a snag.

The largest producer of cars, Henry Ford, had the least to gain by better roads. His Model "T" was not designed for good roads and he realized that his sales would drop off if roads were improved. He refused to modernize, or re-design, or phase out the Model "T" so he pulled out of the project without public explanation. Henry Ford knew that his money was essential to the project if it were to succeed and that he therefore held life or death power over it. In fitting with his personality, he chose death to the project. Apparently, he realized that he would not

The Jeffery Quad

Drives, Brakes and Steers on All Four Wheels

Efficient in War—Economical in Peace

The Jeffery Quad

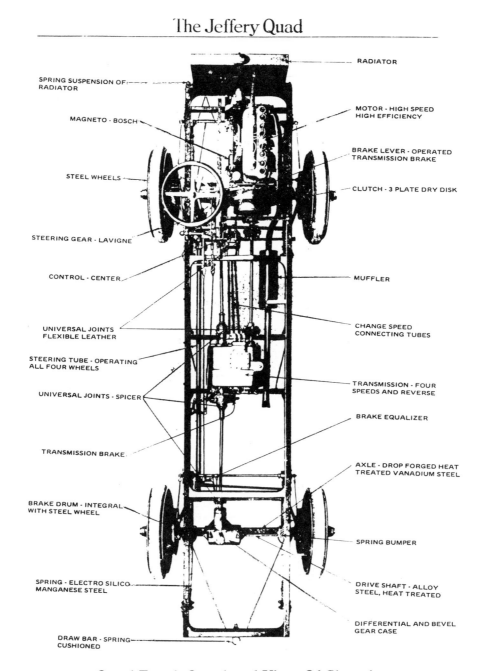

RADIATOR

SPRING SUSPENSION OF RADIATOR

MOTOR - HIGH SPEED HIGH EFFICIENCY

MAGNETO - BOSCH

BRAKE LEVER - OPERATED TRANSMISSION BRAKE

STEEL WHEELS

CLUTCH - 3 PLATE DRY DISK

STEERING GEAR - LAVIGNE

CONTROL - CENTER

MUFFLER

UNIVERSAL JOINTS FLEXIBLE LEATHER

CHANGE SPEED CONNECTING TUBES

STEERING TUBE - OPERATING ALL FOUR WHEELS

UNIVERSAL JOINTS - SPICER

TRANSMISSION - FOUR SPEEDS AND REVERSE

BRAKE EQUALIZER

TRANSMISSION BRAKE

AXLE - DROP FORGED HEAT TREATED VANADIUM STEEL

BRAKE DRUM - INTEGRAL WITH STEEL WHEEL

SPRING BUMPER

SPRING - ELECTRO SILICO MANGANESE STEEL

DRIVE SHAFT - ALLOY STEEL, HEAT TREATED

DIFFERENTIAL AND BEVEL GEAR CASE

DRAW BAR - SPRING CUSHIONED

Quad Truck Overhead View Of Chassis

Overhead view shows how engine is set off to the right side of the chassis. Power from the engine goes straight through the clutch and transmission and transfer case with front and rear drive shafts coming out of the transfer case in straight lines for minimum power loss.

Rear wheel steering mechanism is also visible. To achieve this arrangement, the steering column had to be at a 90 degree right angle to the frame, instead of on a slant as in a passenger car.

Quad Four Wheel Steering

Photo showing four wheel steering which allowed such a long heavy vehicle to make a very tight turn. Looking closely at the photo, it can be seen that the front edge of the front tires point to the left while the front edge of the rear tires point to the right.

1914 Ford With A Flat Tire

The gentleman's expression indicates he would probably rather be doing something else, almost anything else, than patching this inner tube. The tire is a "clincher" type where the bead of the tire fits into the groove on the outer rim of the wheel. Getting the tire off or on the rim was no easy job, especially when it had to be done in the middle of the road, as shown here. One look at the jagged objects on the road, and the condition of the road, explains why so many tires were punctured. Rather than be forced to repair a tire the way this man is doing, some owners paid a little extra to get demountable rims. They could carry a good tire, already mounted and inflated, and then merely change rims when a tire went flat. The flat tire could be patched later, at a more convenient place than by the side of the road.

After this man gets the inner tube patched, he has to put it back into the tire, then get the tire back onto the rim properly without pinching the inner tube, then pump air into the tube. The pump is shown laying down behind the car. In this case the tire and inner tube could be

(Caption Continued)

patched successfully. Spares were carried for times when the tire would be damaged beyond repair, or needed fixing at the side of the road. Badly damaged tires could have a section vulcanized in, thus saving the tire. Since the cars didn't travel all that fast, out of balance vibrations were not noticed on patched or vulcanized tires.

This car has two spare tires; a close look will reveal that one spare is slightly taller than the other. The front size on this Ford was 30 x 3 which was 24" diameter, the rear size was 30 x 3 1/2 which was 23" diameter. The reason they are placed where they are is that there is no door there; the driver had to enter or exit from the right front door. The spare tires were accessories. Another accessory was the round trunk which fit inside the tire opening.

Having two license tags was necessary in some areas, as one state, or D.C. would not recognize license tags from another state. Even the Presidential White House cars had license tags from Maryland and Virginia as well as D.C. It wasn't until the mid 1920's that all states passed reciprocal agreements allowing cars into their state's displaying some other state's tag.

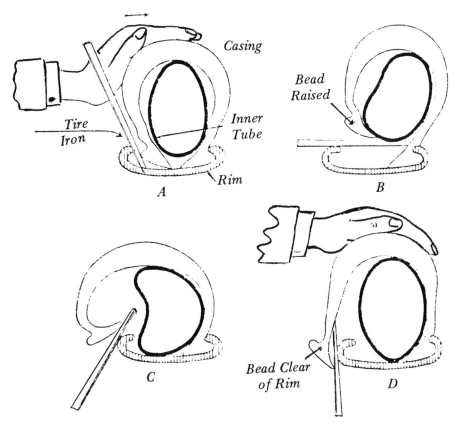

Changing A Clincher Tire

Cross section drawing show how a clincher tire was removed from the rim. One had to take *extreme* care not to pinch the inner tube which actually held the air pressure. Until it was learned by experience, it was quite possible to pinch an inner tube while either removing or re-installing a tire. Often one was not aware of a pinched tube until trying to pump air into it, after it was back on the rim. Having to go through all this at the side of the road could be quite frustrating.

1914 Electric

This photo shows an electric connected to the battery charger. Both front and rear hump covers are open to gain access to all the batteries. This scene is quite unusual as it shows a country setting with the car outside. These vehicles were mostly driven around town and kept inside a garage of some sort overnight while on the charger.

An extremely unusual accessory is shown with this electric, a spare tire. These cars were usually not driven where they would get a puncture or a blowout. This spare appears to have most of its original wrapping still on, so apparently it has not been needed as yet.

be personally glorified, the way he was with the $5.00 a day wage or the winning of the Selden Patent case, because he would only be one of several participants. He also realized that if the project failed, Roy Chapin, as head of it, would be the one who failed, so Henry Ford let it fall.

1915

Budd And Dodge Form A Unique Arrangement

This was the first year of production for the Dodge Brothers car as it was called. It was quite a "Plain Jane" in looks, but ruggedly built for its day. One of its innovations was something just barely out of the experimental stage, the all steel body. It was built for Dodge by the Budd Company.

Until now, all body manufacturing had "evolved" from buggy and wagon types and styles. Instead of being all wood, most car bodies now had a wood frame with panels of sheet metal nailed over them. Carriages and buggies had been made with wood panels nailed over a wooden frame, so everyone stayed with the same basic idea. Old wagon builders, like Fisher and Studebaker, had large investments in forests and wood working machinery, etc.

The Budd Company, on the other hand, was new to the body building business, having begun in 1910. They had made a few experimental bodies for Oakland and Cadillac of General Motors, who also had a substantial investment in wood working machinery and trained workers, etc. The established companies could not justify the expense involved in re-training all their body builders from wood to steel, in addition to the remodeling of plants, and the investments in new tools and equipment, to build all steel bodies.

The arrangements worked out between Budd and the Dodge Brothers were unique. Budd agreed to supply bodies to Dodge at a certain price for a year, then both companies would go over Budd's books. If the profits were excessive, Budd would reduce prices accordingly; if the profits were too low, the price would be raised by the proper amount.

Since Budd had not built bodies on as large a scale as Dodge expected to require, neither company was exactly sure what a fair price would be. Dodge wanted the Budd arrangement to be long lasting, because it realized the advantages of the all-steel body over a wood-framed body, and because they realized that the only way Budd could furnish them would be if Budd made a profit.

Dodge did not want to use the all-steel body as a selling point for strength and freedom from rattles and squeaks for a few years, then have to look for another supplier. There were no other suppliers of all-steel bodies in the foreseeable future. For a while, competitors referred to the Budd-built bodies of Dodge Brothers as tin can bodies.

It was the custom in those days for auto makers in the medium price range, such as Dodge, to furnish a spare rim on which the owner could have a spare tire installed along with an inner tube and a flap, but the tire, as well as the inner tube and the flap, were all considered accessories. It was quite common for advertising pictures to show only a spare rim, so as not to mislead anyone to think that a spare tire was part of the standard equipment. The publicity photo of the very first Dodge Brothers touring car to leave the assembly line has John and Horace themselves in the rear seat, looking proper and dignified for the occasion — but with only a spare rim and not a spare tire on the car.

Cadillac Modernizes With A V-8

While Cadillac was having its legal setbacks with the two-speed rear axle in 1914, Henry Leland and Charles Kettering and the Cadillac engineers had been working on a secret project that would take the automobile business by storm. In 1915, Cadillac brought out their first V-8 engine. It was a tremendous success. There had been other V-8 engines, some of which had been in European cars, and one V-8 had been an aircraft engine. None were low enough in price to be able to sell in any quantity at all. What the Cadillac engineers did, under the leadership of Leland and Kettering, was to get everything so it worked properly — something which none of the previous attempts at V-8's had been able to do. Cadillac also converted to left-side drive and designed an entirely new, modern, chassis to go with its V-8 engine and new streamlined bodies.

Within six months of the introduction of the Cadillac V-8, Packard introduced a V-12 engine. They had been making a six-cylinder engine for several years and called their new V-12 the twin-six and the other one the single six. The idea of eight cylinders, such as Cadillac had just brought out, especially in "V" form, was very different to most car buyers. Packard wisely decided to keep the familiar idea of "six" in their "twin six" name. Both Cadillac and Packard cars, with their "V" engines, were excellent for their times but they were not really competitors until many years later.

Packard and Pierce-Arrow were competitors as both were prestige cars. Cadillac would be what an executive on his way up might buy. When he "arrived", he would consider a Packard or a Pierce-Arrow. At this time Pierce-Arrow was still making six-cylinder cars, although Cadillac is said to have made many of Pierce-Arrow's rear axle parts during the World War I era. But the end did not come for quite a few years. The decision by Pierce-Arrow to stick with a six-cylinder engine at a time when Cadillac went to a V-8 and Packard went to a V-12, was the ultimate un-doing of Pierce-Arrow. Pierce-Arrow was at its peak in 1915; Cadillac and Packard were still advancing.

Packard, Cadillac, And Dodge Are The Icing On The Cake

Three automobile achievements happened this year to make it generally conceded to be the year when the United States was definitely ahead of Europe in automobile development. The U.S.A. had been gradually advancing due to the effects of two major economic factors in car sales' appeal to its potential customers: (1) The ordinary working man could forsee the day when he would have his own car, whereas, in Europe, such an idea was still far beyond the financial dreams of most workers. (2) There was a concerted effort in the United States to build several different brands of cars which the ordinary working man could afford or for which he could plan ahead; nothing like this marketing consideration existed anywhere in Europe.

The immediate success of the Packard twin six (V-12), the Cadillac V-8, and the "Plain Jane" Dodge Brothers touring car — all introduced in 1915 — proved to the world that the United States of America had the right combination of success factors. The engineering, the design, the planning, and the marketing of all those three cars, in particular, amounted to the icing on the cake. Until 1905 to 1907, the U.S.A. was running second to Europe in automobile development, except in the area of steam car development, when the Stanley Steamer won the Dewar Cup in 1906, at over 120 M.P.H., and even bettered this in 1907, at over 180 M.P.H. At that same time, also, the cars chosen by the White House for President Theodore Roosevelt's personal transportation were White Steamers. Then the gap narrowed until about 1910 when the U.S. and Europe became pretty close, if not equal, in automobile development. By 1915, it had to be agreed by all concerned that Europe was not able to match the United States in all aspects that were required to get a variety of excellent cars, for their time, on the market in large enough quantities to make them financially successful.

This 1915 ad refers to the newly-formed Lincoln Highway Association's plan to build a coast to coast road system. It was not possible to drive all the way across the United States in 1915 on paved roads. The system was named for President Abraham Lincoln who had encouraged the railroads in the early 1860's to build a coast to coast railway system.

Source: *National Auto History Collection
of the Detroit Public Library*

John and Horace Dodge in the first Dodge Brothers automobile. Car has a spare rim, but no spare tire mounted on it.

The Packard 1-35 Phaeton

ANNOUNCING THE *Packard* "TWIN-SIX"

A twelve-cylinder car
that recasts every motor-car standard and that revises all previous
ideas of motor-car sufficiency

By a rapidity of pick-up, a range of high-gear activity,
an ease of hill-climbing, a sureness of sustained speed
and a nicety of control never before combined in
any motor car, it is *the absolute master of every situation and the perfect servant of every driver.*

CHASSIS IN TWO LENGTHS. The I-35 — wheel-base, 135 inches.
The I-25 — wheel-base, 125 inches. Descriptive Literature on request.

PACKARD MOTOR CAR COMPANY, DETROIT
Contributor to Lincoln Highway

**The first series of the famous Packard Twin-Six. It was quite an engineering
masterpiece in its day.**

A New Power Plant
for the Pierce-Arrow

THE Pierce-Arrow has a new engine of greater power. This engine has been developed by Pierce-Arrow engineers. They have named it The Dual Valve Engine.

The increased power it yields adds to the comfort and convenience of the Pierce-Arrow Car. This comfort and convenience are enhanced by the perfect control. With the new engine one can go from five miles an hour to seventy and back again to five on high gear. This almost eliminates the necessity of shifting gears—either on hills or in traffic.

It offers more power with no greater weight, more speed with less gasoline, more flexibility with less gear shifting. It is cooler, quieter and quicker than any previous Pierce-Arrow.

The new engine is no sudden innovation. It is the result of years of careful experiment. It is in line with the steady development of the Pierce-Arrow. It is in harmony with the policy that no changes should be made until a real improvement had been perfected.

Pierce-Arrow

THE PIERCE-ARROW MOTOR CAR CO.
BUFFALO, N. Y.

1918 ad shows that Pierce-Arrow's answer to Cadillac's V-8 and Packard's twin six (V-12), and to several other V-8 and V-12 engines, was to make their six-cylinder engine a little more complicated by making it with two sets of valves per cylinder. They retained their basic slow speed engine design, however, while Packard and Cadillac were advancing considerably.

Source: *National Auto History Collection
of the Detroit Public Library*

1915 Cadillac V-8 Touring Car

Model "T" Ford Assembly Line

The chassis as shown here appears to be complete and in running condition, possibly only needing oil, water, and gasoline to actually run. The next step is for side aprons and a body to be installed, then fenders and hood and lights. Whichever body style the particular chassis received, the large round object, the gas tank, will be under the front seat. The seat cushion will have to be removed thousands of times during the life of the car to put in the gas.

The brass radiator, the tall wooden dashboard, and tires with no tread identify this as 1916, or possibly 1915 or 1914. A close look shows the emergency brake handle pulled back all the way. This put the planetary transmission in neutral, through a system of levers, so that the rear tires would roll when they reached the tracks ahead.

The large overhead pulleys and belts, primitive by modern standards, were the latest innovations in this era for transmitting mechanical power from a central location.

1915 Chevrolet Roadster

This model was known as the AMESBURY SPECIAL and was a much sportier version of the regular 1915 Chevrolet. Wire wheels were available as accessories, but the original owner of this car did not choose to buy them.

1915 was when the company was still under Mr. Durant's control exclusively after Mr. Louis Chevrolet was no longer with the company which had his name, yet before Chevrolet became part of General Motors.

Durant Uses Chevrolet Motor Co. To Take Back General Motors

Chevrolet, under Durant's guidance, expanded production facilities and was able to sell all the 15,000 cars it produced in 1915. Had Durant concentrated on Chevrolet production in the same way that Henry Ford had concentrated on Model "T" production, it would have been quite a contest. Instead, Durant, ever the wheeler and dealer, began the drive to regain control of General Motors.

General Motors had not paid its stock holders any dividends since the bankers took over late in 1910. The directors of G.M. had concentrated on getting the company onto a sensible business-like basis and using the profits to pay off the huge bank loans, and to expand and keep on top of the latest ideas. The self-starter, the Buick six-cylinder engine, the Cadillac V-8, and the switch to left hand drive of all General Motors cars had all been planned and carried out while the bankers were in control. When Charles W. Nash was president of General Motors, G.M. stock was selling at about $82.00 a share in the beginning of 1915.

Durant began making moves to regain control of General Motors. He convinced the bankers who had loaned him the two-and-three-quarter million to get Chevrolet production started in 1914, to come into a partnership with him. The idea was to buy up all the General Motors stock that was available and turn it over to Durant to control. They needed help and convinced Pierre S. DuPont to join with them. Durant also got friends and other DuPont people to buy up G.M. stock to let Durant control. Durant had a lot of friends who could see that he was having success with his new Chevrolet company. He convinced them to trade their G.M. stock, which they had been holding on to, for some of Durant's Chevrolet stock at the rate of five Chevrolet shares for one General Motors share. It just so happened that the G.M. Board of Directors meeting was scheduled for September 16, 1915, exactly seven years to the day after Durant had secretly formed General Motors. Durant knew that the five-year voting trust that the bankers had insisted upon back in 1910 would be over on October 1, when the last of the debt to the bankers would be paid. He also knew that at this September 16 board meeting, the board would vote to pay the final amount of the loan; they would also nominate new directors. Since Durant had remained a director of G.M. all these years, he was able to attend this directors' meeting. The outcome was that Durant gained control of, or already owned, over 50% of all General Motors stock, and thereby controlled General Motors.

Maxwell Sponsors Eddie Rickenbacker

The Maxwell company thought it would boost sales if they sponsored some race cars. The driver who was Maxwell's star this year and also in 1916 was Eddie Rickenbacker.

Charles T. Jeffery Survives The Lusitania Sinking

Charles T. Jeffery, president of the firm his father founded to build Rambler cars, had a frightening experience. He sailed on the Lusitania from New York in May. Cunard had equipped this ship with high-powered naval rifles and it was listed by the British Navy as an auxiliary cruiser. When it set sail from New York, it carried about six million pounds of ammunition. Jeffery disregarded all common sense by sailing on this ship since the German government had run large ads in New York newspapers telling prospective passengers that the ship would be going into a war zone around Great Britain and was "subject to destruction" and that people traveling there "do so at their own risk". Mr. Jeffery was one of the fortunate survivors.

The Most Famous Ad Appears

This was the year when there appeared one of the most famous ads in history, whether in automobile advertising or in other areas. It was suggested by Wilfred Leland and actually written by Theodore Mac Manus who handled Cadillac advertising at the time. "The Penalty of Leadership" did not mention Cadillac's name or, for that matter, even mention so much as an automobile. The closest they came was to say a "manufactured product". The only way a reader had of knowing who paid for the ad was the word "Cadillac" in the border of the ad. The last sentence says: "That which deserves to live — lives".

Studebaker Designs Its Second Car

In 1915, the only surviving one of the five Studebaker brothers, John, was now past 80 and had been president of the company for over a dozen years. He retired and shortly afterward Studebaker itself designed its first car since the electric of 1902. It had observed the good and bad points of the cars it had been assembling since that time, so it had a pretty good idea of what to do and what to avoid.

Their efforts resulted in a reasonably good medium-priced car, but their reputation of over 65 years in business had more to do with selling their cars than it did with the quality of the cars themselves.

1916

Nash Bows Out Of General Motors As Durant Resumes Control

Durant was still operating General Motors and Chevrolet as two separate companies which, in fact, is really what they were all the time. Actually, in order to get Chevrolet production under way two years before, Durant had granted licenses to several concerns around the country, to make, or to assemble, Chevrolet cars. They were all made the same, but they were also the pride of the local area people who were employed to build them. Many other car makers had plants of different types located throughout the country, but they were not part locally owned as was the Chevrolet setup. Everyone, including Durant, realized that sooner or later Chevrolet would become part of General Motors. He now set out to consolidate all the plants under his control so that when the merger did come, he, Durant, would have an excellent organization to sell to his fellow General Motors directors.

By the early part of the year, most of the directors who had been placed on the G.M. board by the bankers in 1910 were now gone. Durant tried, without success, to convince Charles W. Nash to remain as General Motors' president.

Mr. Nash recalled how Mr. Dort and Mr. Durant had taken him in when he was just a teenager and had given him a job in their carriage factory; and then constantly promoted him; and how Durant even suggested him for his present position as President of General Motors. Nash's conservative and business like nature blended well with the bankers on the board of directors during the past years and he wanted to keep on friendly terms with everyone. He knew Durant's nature was such that he had to be in charge and he foresaw possible clashes ahead.

Source: *National Auto History Collection
of the Detroit Public Library*

Charles W. Nash

Ransom E. Olds was in several businesses during his very active lifetime. First was the Olds Motor Works with the Oldsmobile cars. Then, using his initials, he formed the REO Motor Car Company. By 1916, he was into power lawn mowers.

For a long time, Mr. Nash had wanted a car with his own name on it. He resigned from General Motors and one of his banker friends helped him buy the Jeffery Co. of Kenosha. The name of the cars and truck was soon changed to "Nash".

Henry Ford Antagonizes The Dodge's Into Filing Suit

Henry Ford decided to stop paying dividends of the Ford Motor Co. to the stock holders and instead put the profits back into the Ford Motor Co. for expansion. Maybe G.M. not paying stock holders for five years and putting the money into modernization and paying off the bank loans had some influence on Ford. The River Rouge plant was his current project and he was also attempting to build a cheap farm tractor which would use as many Model "T" parts as possible. All the stock holders objected; the Dodge brothers demanded 10% of the profits since they still owned 10% of the Ford Motor Co., Henry Ford refused. The Dodge brothers sued for $20 million which is what they calculated their 10% of the profits to be. The case dragged on for several years.

Pancho Villa Is Used To Test Mechanized Warfare

The United States military had their hands full along the Mexican border with Pancho Villa. General Pershing used this opportunity to test a number of makes of cars and trucks in the hot, sandy, roadless conditions of the area. Two makes of cars and one make of truck, which we have been discussing, proved equal to the task: the Dodge Brothers touring car, the Cadillac touring car, and the Jeffery/Nash Quad truck. Many others, whose names are no longer household words, distinguished themselves also. The first mechanized cavalry charge in U.S. Army history took place in 1916 against Pancho Villa. The U.S. Army was using Dodge Brothers' touring cars and the attack was led by one of General Pershing's junior officers, lieutenant George Patton.

Wilson's Re-Election Invites U.S. Into Europe's War

Politics has played a tremendous role in changing the history and culture of the United States. It is appropriate to discuss it here briefly as automobile history was also greatly influenced by it. The war in Europe was coming to pretty much of a stalemate. Both sides were about equally matched militarily and financially. Each side in Europe was probably to blame for the war. The Allies accused the Central Powers of building a war machine. The Central Powers accused the Allies of exploiting people all over the world in the form of colonies; the U.S. had been a British colony less than 140 years before. The saying that the sun never set on the British Empire was very true in 1916; the French and Dutch still had many colonies all around the world in 1916.

Several of the super rich bankers in New York had loaned money to England and were not about to kiss it all "goodbye". What was needed was an excuse to bring the United States into the war on the side of England. The Republicans nominated Charles Evans Hughes and the Democrats nominated the incumbent, Woodrow Wilson. They encouraged President Wilson to keep everyone stirred up by the "He kept us out of war" slogan. Had he campaigned on domestic issues, he would have had to explain the graduated income tax and also the Federal Reserve System, both of which came into being during the first administration.

President Wilson was re-elected by a whisker. It wasn't until the California results came in close to midnight on election night that the Wilson victory was definite. Republican candidate Hughes had retired for the evening confident that he had beaten the president.

The super-rich controlled many leading newspapers around the country. The editorial policy was immediately switched, right after the election, to the theme of "sooner or later we will be in it".

1917

Brass Radiators No Longer Seen On New Fords

The Model "T" Ford took on a different appearance with the change of the outer radiator rim from all-brass to all-steel, painted black. The car had evolved somehat in many relatively minor changes during the eight years of its production. This change seemed to be a turning point as one had to look twice, to get used to the changes and to make sure the car actually was a Ford.

DuPont Invests Heavily In General Motors Stock

This was somewhat of an interim year for General Motors and William C. Durant, who was still wheeling and dealing as much as ever with money he didn't have. Durant neglected to inform the DuPont stockholders of many of his plans for G.M. The DuPonts were busy selling their gun powder for World War I and didn't concern themselves with General Motors or with Durant for a while.

However, G.M. stock dropped off and DuPont needed some place to invest the profits it was making from the war. It knew Durant's ideas were expensive to say the least; but DuPont also realized that G.M. could benefit by the sensible business manner of the DuPont Co. experience; so DuPont bought 25% control of General Motors and put its treasurer, John Jacob Raskob, on the G.M. board of directors.

Durant Underestimates Henry Leland's Patriotism

One of Durant's big errors in judgement came this year. Henry M. Leland had known, ever since his 1910 vacation trip to Europe, that a big war was coming, and when the United States entered the war, he knew the only "aeroplanes" this country had were a few French built aircraft. The LIBERTY aeroplane engine had been developed mainly by Mr. Jesse G. Vincent who was also the engineer for the Packard V-12 a couple of years earlier.

Henry Leland asked permission of Durant to convert some of Cadillac's facilities to making the LIBERTY aircraft engine.

The aircraft industry in this country, in 1917, had no mass production facilities and it would be up to the automobile industry to produce any item needed by aircraft in large quantities and still maintain the standards of high quality most important to aircraft. However, Durant said "No". He was a pacifist and didn't want to get involved in war production. Leland tried, but without success, to change Durant's "No" answer.

Because of love of country, Henry Leland resigned from Cadillac and from General

Motors and started his own company with the purpose of manufacturing the LIBERTY engine. He named his new company after the man for whom he had tremendous respect, who was also the candidate for President for whom Henry Leland had first voted — LINCOLN. Back in 1864, Abraham Lincoln was running for his second term when Henry Leland was 23.

When Henry Leland resigned from Cadillac, so did his son Wilfred, and quite a few engineers and other executives and employees. Very soon, Durant realized his mistake and asked the Leland's to return; but they declined as they were already involved in the LINCOLN MOTOR COMPANY.

Several of the automobile manufacturers of that year soon pooled their talents and resources and facilities to produce the Liberty aircraft engines and other wartime materials. Among them were Packard, Lincoln, Cadillac, Buick, Dodge, Ford, along with several others whose names are no longer houehold words. They were all competitors in the automobile business, but since most knew each other, in this war time period, they all banded together for the common good of the country in this emergency time.

World War I Is The Cover For Financial Investors In Russia

It is difficult to see history while you are living it. Such was the case with the majority of these citizens, including Henry Leland, Jesse Vincent, and the rest of the automobile manufacturers and their employees. They did what they considered to be their patriotic duty, without realizing that they had been set up by the super rich — and the bankers through their influence on the President. As soon as the election was over and Woodrow Wilson was re-elected to a second term, the super-rich controlled newspapers took a turnabout approach.

It now became only a matter of time until the United States would be brought into Europe's War. The sinking of the Lusitania on May 7, 1915, 18 months before the election, was re-hashed to raise emotions against anything German. The propaganda succeeded, with the United States declaring War on Germany on April 6, just barely a month after President Wilson's second inauguration, on March 4.

Possibly not even the President was aware of the extent to which the super-rich were willing to go. Russia was about to have a political upheaval. Although Russia was allied with England and France, and with the U.S.A., and was keeping part of the German Army busy, Czar Nicholas II abdicated in March, before the United States declared War on Germany, but only after the capital city of Petrograd had riots with food supplies exhausted and factories closed. One provisional government toppled and a second such government followed, granting a general amnesty to about a quarter of a million political prisoners, including Communists and others anxious to overthrow the existing government.

While this was occurring, a newspaper reporter for a Communist paper on New York's lower East Side set out for Russia. His name was Trotsky and he was going to meet Lenin. Where was Lenin? He had been in exile for twelve years and was then in Switzerland. The super-rich bankers of Germany gave him five million in gold and got him through war torn Europe on a "sealed train".

When it was discovered that one of the super-rich Germans was Max Warbug, his brother, Paul, resigned his position on the United States Federal Reserve Board at once. Paul Warbug's father-in-law was another super-rich banker, Jacob Schiff, who came out and boasted that the Russian Revolution had succeeded in 1917, primarily due to his money being behind it. He underwrote Trotsky. One of Jacob Schiff's descendants revealed, over thirty years later, that about $20 million had been "invested" in the Russian Revolution by Jacob. In 1917, Russia did not have a central bank but the super-rich bankers would very soon remedy that situation. The super-rich controlled Lenin and Trotsky. Once again, they were financing both sides of the same war.

Source: *National Auto History Collection
of the Detroit Public Library*

Liberty Engine On Test Stand

Henry Leland, with white beard and in vest, and son Wilfred Leland in suit and bow tie. Note "Packard" pennant behind Henry.

Pipes coming out of top center of engine, and also along floor, carry cooling water to outside radiator, not visible in photo.

Type Of Plane Using "Liberty" Engine

MARMON 34

The experience gained, and the organization developed, in building the Liberty Motor for the United States Government, has enabled this Company to produce a motor car built to the accuracy and "close limits" attained for the first time in Liberty Motor production. Advanced design and preciseness in manufacture accomplish new results in power, smoothness, economy, and long life.

NORDYKE & MARMON COMPANY
Established 1851 :: :: INDIANAPOLIS

MARMON was one of the countless auto makers, whose names are no longer household words. They were proud to be one of the companies that converted a great part of their facilities to war production work during World War I. This 1920 ad suggests that their newly learned precision techniques enabled them to build better post-war cars. Marmon ceased production during the depression of the early 1930's. A spin off of the original Nordyke & Marmon Co., founded in 1851, is in existence today, known as Marmon-Herrington. Among other things, Marmon-Herrington coverts big heavy duty trucks to four-wheel drive for off-the-road usage.

1918 World War I Army Tank

This tank was built by Ford. Power was from two Model "T" engines and transmissions, one for each track. The war ended before mass production could get under way; only about six were built. Since this vehicle was so small, steel extension skids were fitted to the front to try to prevent the vehicle from tipping over when crossing a big shell hole likely to be found on a battlefield.

1918

Walter Marr And C. H. Wills Leave Their Respective Jobs

Each of the two brilliant engineers, largely responsible for the success of two of the pioneer companies, left his job this year. After 17 years, Walter Marr, who had been the brains behind the early Buick Company when Mr. Buick was just getting started in 1901, decided to retire.

The other brilliant engineer was C. H. Wills, who had done considerable design work on the first Fordmobile. When Henry Ford was too poor to buy coal for his stove, he and C. H. Wills would each put on boxing gloves and spar to get the blood circulating in their fingers again, so that they could keep on at the drawing boards. It was C. H. Wills who developed the way to make vanadium steel cheap enough and in large enough quantities to be practical for the automobile. Now, however, the Model "T" was not going to be changed a great deal. There was an engineering and design department at Ford, but it was mainly occupied with ways of making the Model "T" cheaper to produce. C. H. Wills was frustrated; he wanted to go on to newer things than being tied down indefinitely with the Model "T" Ford. He resigned to eventually build a car with his own name on it, but it is one of the forgotten names now. He then joined the Chrysler Corporation as an engineer and remained there the rest of his working years. C. H. Wills was another of those working for Henry Ford who knew him when he was poor, but now, he too was out of Henry Ford's life.

Maxwell And Chalmers Make A Five Year Agreement

At the Maxwell Company, a strange set of circumstances was taking place. Maxwell had been one of the top five or six selling brands of cars since their re-organization in 1914, and their decision to concentrate on one small, low-priced car. However, since their plants and machinery were now rather out dated, Maxwell got together with Hugh Chalmers who made the Chalmers car. The Chalmers car was formerly known as the Chalmers-Detroit and was one of the companies with which Roy Chapin was involved, before he helped start the Hudson Motor Car Co. in 1909. The Chalmers factory was modern and excellent, but its cars weren't selling all that well. Chalmers cars were priced in the medium range, which was already saturated with several fairly good brands of cars. The result of all this was that Maxwell cars would now be built in the Chalmers factory, and that the Chalmers cars would be sold through Maxwell dealers. Each company still remained independent, however, and the companies drew up an agreement to continue this arrangement for five years.

Francis E. Stanley Succumbs To Auto Accident Injuries

The Stanley twins were now 68 and were considering selling the company they had originally founded twenty years earlier, and retiring. Francis E. was a bit more of a hot-rodder than his twin brother. Their two cylinder steam engine cars, still with only 25 moving parts in the engine, could out-run any ordinary gasoline engine car. One day, F. E. came up over the crest of a hill to find a farmer's hay wagon blocking the entire road. It was either hit the load of hay or run off the road. He chose not to jeopardize the life of the farmer and went off the road. He wasn't killed instantly, but died later of his injuries. Freelan O. Stanley was deeply grieved by his twin brother's death and sold the company soon afterwards. He eventually

FINER

C. Harold Wills has designed and built in the Wills Sainte Claire a motor car that is lighter, swifter, safer, more economical, more comfortable, more durable and finer—a motor car, not more complicated, but greatly simplified. Have you ridden in the Wills Sainte Claire?

C. H. Wills & Company, *Marysville, Michigan*

WILLS SAINTE CLAIRE
Motor Cars

© C. H. W. Co.

made violins, while remaining in a capacity resembling consultant emeritus to the new owners of the car company. He survived to the age of 92, passing away in 1940. He lived longer than any of the U.S. auto pioneers who had a car named for himself.

Henry Ford Runs For The U.S. Senate

Henry Ford ran for the U.S. Senate in 1918 as a Democrat. Truman Newberry was elected the winner, however. As it turned out, Mr. Newberry was accused of doing some naughty things concerning election frauds and was never allowed to assume the duties of Senator from Michigan. The governor of Michigan appointed former Detroit Mayor and former Ford Co. Business Manager, James Couzens as Senator from Michigan.

Since there were only 48 states in 1918, there were only 96 senators. It just so happened that there would have been 48 Republicans and 48 Democrats, had Henry Ford been elected. Since the Vice President of the United States is also President of the Senate, he votes when there is a tie. Like President Wilson, Vice President Marshall was also a Democrat. Had Democrat, Henry Ford been elected Senator from Michigan, Republican Henry Cabot Lodge, Sr. would probably have not been chairman of the Committee on Foreign Relations during the debates on the League of Nations and the Versailles Treaty.

But the thought of someone with a disposition like Henry Ford's becoming a United States Senator is too frightening to consider further.

Many Car Makers Use V-8 And V-12 Engines For A While

Both Chevrolet and Oldsmobile had V-8 engines this year in addition to their respective four-cylinder models. By now there were about a dozen brands of cars on the market with V-8 and V-12 engines. V-8 power was not too popular in the Chevrolet, so the V-8 was dropped by Chevrolet after slightly over a year. Oldsmobile kept its V-8 engine for a few more of its model years, however.

Durant's Power Is At Its Peak

1918 was the highest point in Durant's life. Never again would he be in complete control of the events around him, or be this successful. The DuPonts had been too busy to keep an eye on him or on G.M. While the DuPonts had installed their own man, John Jacob Rascob, as head of the Finance Committee on the G.M. board, he was fascinated by Durant's grand ideas. Raskob's actions actually encouraged Durant's wheeler and dealer methods. Durant bought more companies and planned a $50 million expansion program for when ever World War I might end.

1917 Pathfinder V-12

One of the many now forgotten companies which tried to compete with Packard by using a V-12 engine. Packard had the name, and the reputation, and the engineering, and the production facilities, and the dealer organization which the small companies like this Pathfinder could not begin to match.

Sedan . . . 2610 lbs. $2950.00	Cabriolet . . 2485 lbs. $2850.00	Brougham . 2575 lbs. $2900.00
Town Car . 2610 lbs. 3200.00	Limousine . 2620 lbs. 3200.00	All Prices F. O. B. Syracuse

FRANKLIN AUTOMOBILE COMPANY
SYRACUSE, N. Y., U. S. A.

Franklin in its hey day, 1917!

This is the center door style, but the posts were not removable so it did not become a hard top as some other center door cars. Since the Franklin had an air-cooled engine, it did not have water or a radiator. This permitted the hood to be made at an angle, or slant. The degree of the slant of the front of the hood resembled a coal shovel turned down. This is why this model Franklin, made for several years, was known as the "shovel nose". A coal shovel was a common item in most households of the era. The pointed windshield, with its four pieces of glass, combined with the slant of the hood which seemed to emphasize the "frog eye" headlights all combined to make this one of the ugliest cars ever made by any manufacturer.

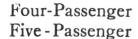

Four-Passenger
Five-Passenger

*Comfort, Power
Style*

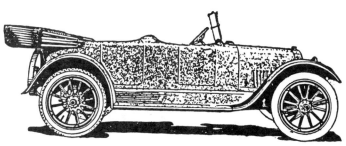

CHEVROLET EIGHT $1385

Chevrolet

The ideal car for
twelve months in
the year. Comfortable in winter.
Delightful in
summer.

490 SEDAN $1060

1918 Chevrolet ad shows a V-8 touring car (with no spare tire) and the four cylinder hard top, shown here with posts removed and all side windows lowered. Some cars, such as this Chevrolet, had the left door at the front for easy driver entry and exit; the right door was in the center and they were still known as center door models.

Two Cars in One
An All-Season Model-Hudson Touring Sedan

HUDSON MOTOR CAR COMPANY, DETROIT, MICHIGAN

This 1915 Hudson is another example of an open hard top with the windows lowered and posts removed, also the center-door style having no front doors. Most Hudsons were not chauffeur driven, nor did their owners normally wear formal cutaway attire. In 1919 Hudson began to change the way this country lived by introducing their low priced Essex sedan.

Source: *National Auto History Collection
of the Detroit Public Library*

1918 Maxwell Center Door Sedan

Hudson And Dodge Brothers Showroom

Hudsons, along the wall at the left of the picture, are the highest priced cars; the Dodge Brothers cars, along the wall at the right of the picture are the medium priced cars. They were not direct competitors, but the higher priced Dodge Brothers overlapped the lower priced Hudson in price. The cutaway engine on the stand is a Hudson. Note that the more expensive Hudson was equipped with tread on the front tires, while the Dodge Brothers' cars had only "smooth tread" front tires. The "cathedral" style rear windows were a Dodge Brothers tradition as seen on the touring car in the photo. The chassis at the rear of the showroom, behind the lamp, is a Dodge Brothers'.

Source: *National Auto History Collection
of the Detroit Public Library*

1917 Dodge Brothers Center Door, Hard Top Sedan With Posts Removed

142

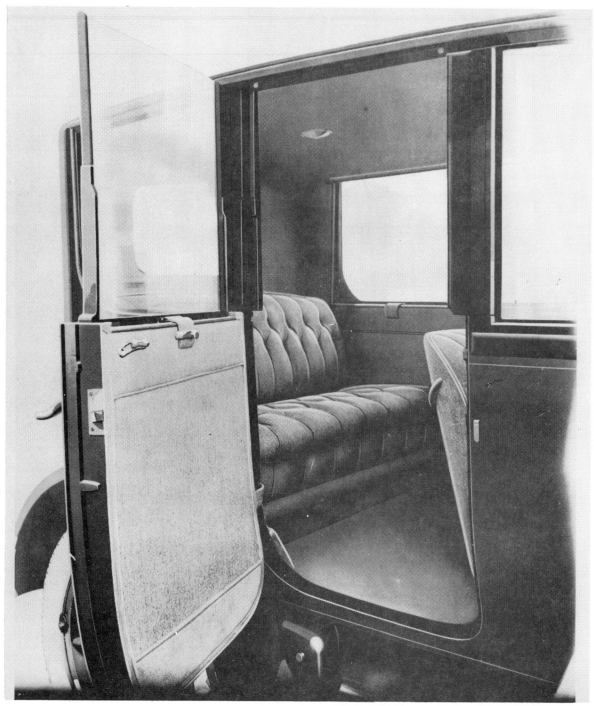

Source: *National Auto History Collection
of the Detroit Public Library*

**1917 Dodge Brothers Center Door Hard Top Sedan Showing
Method Of Retaining Windows**

Inside View Of Dodge Brothers Center Door Hardtop Sedan

Dodge Brothers Center Door Sedan, Hardtop

Inside view shows only one door on each side. Driver and front seat passenger must enter from behind the front seat, walk between the front seats to sit down. Not shown are the gearshift and emergency brake levers which the driver and front passenger must climb around.

While these pictures show the Dodge Brothers version of the center door sedan, all makes of cars, whether with removable posts or permanent, had this same basic floor plan.

DODGE BROTHERS CLOSED CAR

DODGE BROTHERS, DETROIT

Dodge Brothers center door sedan shown with the posts in place, windows raised, and upper section of the windshield opened slightly for ventilation. All side windows could be lowered and posts removed for open air driving. Note that a spare wire wheel is shown, but no tire is mounted on it. Also notice that only rear tires have tread.

Model "T" Ford Center Door Sedan

This was the Ford version of the 1915-1916 center door sedan. The windows could be lowered, but the posts could not be removed, as on the Chevrolet, or Hudson, or Dodge Brothers, and other brands. The windows were shown lowered part way to indicate that the car had glass windows and not ising glass side curtains. It also showed that the glass actually went down, inside the body for full ventilation. Some cars had accessory side windows which merely slid back half way allowing very little air to circulate. This Ford, and other low priced sedans, used straps to raise or lower the window. Crank type window regulators did not become common until the 1920's.

Bohnet detachable limousine top detached

Bohnet Top Enclosure

A rather awkward excuse for an enclosed car. The standard touring car top was removed and this top was installed in its place. There does not appear to be any way to open the side windows which would make it quite uncomfortable on a warm spring day.

Center Door Sedan Floor Plan

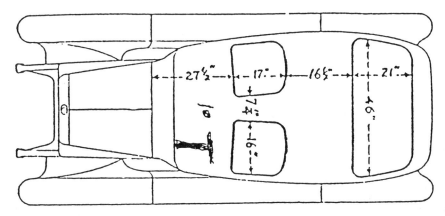

There is plenty of room for five people. You can pass from one compartment to the other between the individual front seats.

Floor plan of a typical "center door sedan", whether open hard top style or fully enclosed type, popular in the United States from about 1915 to about 1920.

1918 Oakland Center Door Sedan

Oakland was a General Motors product. All three windows on each side could be lowered, but the posts were not removable on this Oakland. Wire wheels were an expensive accessory usually installed on the high-priced enclosed cars.

Condition of this car is "un-restored". It would require rebuilding of every mechanical unit of the car, locating missing parts, plus replacement of upholstery, rotted body wood, complete refinishing, etc. at a cost of many thousand dollars.

1919

Durant Underestimates Walter Chrysler's Sincerity

Early in this year, the DuPont's had to pump more money into General Motors. Although, he personally, was not out-and-out in favor of the idea. Durant let the Durant building plans take shape. The building would cost $20 million and Durant would rather have invested that money differently. The building also represented something to him other than his one-man control, as there would now be other executives to do what he had always done by himself.

By his personal meddling, Durant also lost the good services of Walter P. Chrysler as head of Buick. Durant had promised to let Chrysler run Buick, but Durant just couldn't resist making Buick decisions and not letting Chrysler find out about the decisions until later. It happened once too often, and Chrysler resigned from Buick and G.M., and retired. He sold his General Motors stock, and was a millionaire at age forty.

Oregon Invents Gasoline Tax

The State of Oregon discovered that it could add a penny a gallon sales tax onto gasoline prices and have those who used the roads pay for them. Within ten years, all of the other 47 states were also taxing gasoline. Unfortunately, the original Oregon sales tax of a penny a gallon was increased, and, the original Oregon tax concept of using the money only for road building and maintenance, was no longer applied soley to the tax objective. Road building became a secondary tax incentive and the gasoline tax money went into the general treasury of each of the different states.

Henry Ford Tries, But Fails To Trick His Stockholders

Although it had been dragging through the courts for over three years, the Dodge suit against Henry Ford for its un-paid dividends was finally settled in favor of John and Horace Dodge. The settlement cost Henry Ford $20 million which, at the time, was not a great deal of money to him, as the Ford Motor Co. had made over $150 million proft since the Dodge suit was filed.

Henry Ford now decided that he wanted to own all of the original one thousand shares of the Ford Motor Co. stock by himself, so that he would not have to answer to anyone about how the Company was run. He resigned as president, turned everything over to his only child, son Edsel, and then announced that he was going to start a new company to sell a cheaper and better car. Of course it was a lie. He had hopes that the remaining stockholders would panic and rush to un-load their Ford Motor Co. stock which he would secretly buy through third parties.

He hadn't counted on his former business manager and now U.S. Senator, James Couzens' realizing that it was all one big lie. The two biggest remaining groups of stock were owned by James Couzens and the two Dodge brothers. The stock, which had sold for $100.00 a share, sixteen years earlier when the company was founded, now cost Henry Ford $12,500.00 a share, or a total sum of over $100 million to buy all of the outstanding shares back. Approximately $30 million of this amount went to James Couzens for his shares.

Henry Ford now built a home which he named "Fair Lane"; it cost him a million dollars.

The Leland Father And Son Team Decides To Build Another Car

Since the end of the war, the demand for Liberty aircraft engines had ceased and the Lincoln Motor Co. of Mr. Leland existed practically in name only. This was an interim period for the company. It was suggested to the father and son of the Leland team that they use their knowledge, facilities, and the equipment they now had, to build a new car. That sounded like a good idea and the Leland team got busy planning and designing.

One Of The Factors Contributing To "Roaring '20's" Spending

General Motors came up with an idea this year, which turned out to be either very good or very bad, depending on one's point of view. It was the establishment of a retail finance company to allow new cars to be financed directly by General Motors when sold to the customer. It was General Motors Acceptance Corporation and is still known by that name, as well as by its initials G.M.A.C. Until then, most people had to either pay cash for their car purchase, or else arrange their own financing. Banks and loan companies were not over anxious to accept the car itself as security, since it could become wrecked, stolen, abused, or neglected.

At first, only those people with excellent financial standing would be accepted for car loans. The idea of financing the car directly for the consumer allowed General Motors to make a profit from the original sale of the car, as well as from the financing of it. People could now buy a car at once, and pay for it as they drove, instead of saving up to pay cash for it. This allowed G.M. to sell more cars, as no other car manufacturer had anything like G.M.A.C. at the time, and G.M. sold cars from around $600.00 on up, in all price ranges.

The establishment of G.M.A.C. in direct consumer financing was an early step in the easy credit idea of the "Roaring Twenties". The super-rich bankers of the Federal Reserve Board would increase the money supply, and make credit easier and easier to obtain, until the average citizen accepted buying on credit and always being in debt, in order to have right now the luxury items or the necessities which had formerly required planning and saving as a way of life. The process took ten years, from 1919, before the super-rich bankers were able to successfully pull the rug out from underneath the average citizens of the United States and bankrupt them. G.M.A.C. is still in business for one reason and one reason only — it is profitable!

The "Essex" Crackerbox Sedan, By Hudson, Starts A Trend

The Hudson Motor Co., under the leadership of Roy Chapin, had been making good cars in the medium price range for ten years. Now they decided that there were more people who wanted a car, but who couldn't pay Hudson prices, yet they wanted something a lot better than what was available at Ford prices, about $500.00 delivered. As a solution to the public dilemma, Hudson's offering was the Essex.

It had always been possible to buy an enclosed car if you had the money. Ford, Maxwell, Buick, Dodge Brothers, Chevrolet, and all the others, had enclosed cars available, but their price was considerably higher than the open touring car, or the roadster. The main difference in price was due to the fact that a touring car body was only the bottom half of the car, while the top half, consisting of only a folding top and side curtains, was relatively inexpensive to make. Furthermore, because only the wealthy could afford the price of enclosed cars, they were upholstered and trimmed in very fancy materials.

The Hudson idea with the Essex was to build enclosed car comfort, but without the fancy

Source: *National Auto History Collection
of the Detroit Public Library*

Hudson-Essex President Roy Chapin In An Early "Coach".

152

This Challenge to Useless Expense the Greatest Closed Car Issue

You buy a motor car for reliable transportation. You prefer a closed car for comfort. Body accessories and ornaments have little to do with either.

Why pay a huge premium for them?

Within the limits of a moderate-priced closed car you can get only so much. Ornate body-fittings, dome lights, cigar-lighters, clock, vanity cases, etc., add nothing to car performance. They add much to cost.

Essex elects to put the value elsewhere — to build a comfortable, durable closed car of smart appearance—to mount it on the superb Essex chassis, with what American and European experts have called the greatest motor of its size in the world. The rigid, overstrength Essex frame, the smooth positive clutch, the simple controls and strong rear axle are some features of that chassis.

The way it is built explains why Essex cars after 60,000 and 70,000 miles of service are still giving fine, smooth, reliable service. The same idea of utility built the Coach body. It has staunchness and character. It gives the utility of costliest cars. It stays tight and secure.

And isn't its assurance of continued satisfaction and real automobile service more important than showy body extras in the car that is to serve you?

Touring - - $1045   Cabriolet - - $1145   Coach - - $1245
Freight and Tax Extra

ESSEX MOTORS, DETROIT, MICHIGAN

The text of the ad explains the Essex theory of low priced enclosed cars which every other maker of low priced cars eventually copied.

materials or trimmings. They bought their Essex enclosed bodies from Fisher, which was not a General Motors subsidiary at that time. Fisher, however, had a good reputation and good production facilities. Hudson specified that the bodies be as inexpensive as possible with good quality. The result was that the Essex sedan was as square as a crackerbox since the more curves in the body, the more time it took to build and therefore the more expensive it became, due to the additional man hours required. During the first couple of years of the Essex, the only enclosed cars were four door sedans. Essex also built open touring cars and roadsters, however, and a few years later came the two-door Essex sedan. Essex got it to such a point that an enclosed car was just $100.00 above the price of its open touring car.

The general public's reaction was that they were willing to pay the extra money in order to be able to use the car in bad weather all year round. The other car makers saw the success the Essex idea was having, so they, too, came out with low-priced sedans. The availability of easy credit in the 1920's had considerable influence too, but when the Essex was first introduced, only 10% of the cars made in this country were enclosed cars. By 1925, it was 50%, and by 1929, a complete reversal had taken place, so that only 10% were open cars and 90% were enclosed.

1920

Both The Dodge Brothers Are Taken By Death

Personal tragedy struck both the Dodge's this year. They were attending the automobile show in New York City in early January, when Horace caught influenza which developed into pneumonia. John stayed by his brother's bedside but he, too developed pneumonia. Horace eventually recovered, but John died before January was half over. Horace caught influenza again, late in the year, and died while vacationing in Palm Beach, Florida, in December. Ironically, one of the Dodge widows survived to the age of 103.

The Willys' Challenge Lures Chrysler From "Retirement"

Walter P. Chrysler was lured out of retirement by a challenge. The Willys-Overland Company, of Toledo, had been one of the top automobile producers for several years, with its very low-priced Overland, and its medium-priced Willys-Knight. John N. Willys found it necessary to go into debt to the extent of about $50 million, and the bankers approached Chrysler to preserve their interests. Chrysler demanded a million dollars a year salary and a completely free hand to run things. The bankers agreed and signed a two-year contract with Mr. Chrysler.

Durant Is Ousted From G.M. The Final Time

1920 is the year when the end came for good for William C. Durant at General Motors. His one man-control finally caught up with him. The DuPonts tried to get both a Canadian and an English munition firm to buy into General Motors, but the DuPonts couldn't get nearly as

154

John and Horace Dodge in a Formal Photograph

much as was needed. Then the DuPonts went to the J. P. Morgan banking interests, that insisted on buying $25 million in G.M. stock at $10.00 a share, although the current price was over $25.00 a share in the open market. The J. P. Morgan interests also insisted that one of their men be put on the General Motors Board of Directors.

Within just a couple of months after the transaction was completed, the J. P. Morgan interests sold most of their General Motors stock on the open market. This large amount of stock, all at one time, sent the price down to about $20.00 a share, but still gave the J. P. Morgan interests a quick 100% profit on what they sold.

Many of Durant's friends had bought G.M. stock on his personal recommendation. It was legal to buy stock with only 10% down in those days; but many of his friends could not take such a financial loss, so Durant personally bailed them out, by either making up the difference between what they had paid for the stock and what it was worth now, or by buying their stock outright for their original purchase price. Since most of these friends had bought their stock on the advice of Durant, he felt obliged to protect them against such tremendous losses. Durant now became so heavily involved in trying to cover his friends' losses with his own stock, which was now worth a lot less also, that the business of being President of General Motors took a back seat to everything else.

There was a general post war economic let-down, but Durant refused to lower the prices of General Motors cars as other car manufacturers had already done. This, combined with engineering and testing flaws at Oldsmobile, Oakland, and Chevrolet, only made matters worse, and Durant finally agreed to lower G.M. car prices. His personal fortune went down at this time due to the falling G.M. stock prices and to his having covered his friends losses,

The Morgans and the DuPonts did not want General Motors to fail again, so they agreed to buy all of Durant's stock, and pay off all his stock debts, if he would resign from General Motors. Durant could see that there was no other way, so he agreed to resign. This made the second time in ten years that Durant had lost control of General Motors. This was the final time, however, as he was not allowed to remain on the Board of Directors, as the bankers had allowed him to do in 1910.

Gaston Chevrolet, Louis' Brother, Gets A Short Lived Honor

The winner of the Indianapolis 500 Memorial Day race was Gaston Chevrolet, a brother of Louis. Gaston had remained in auto racing after Louis went to work for Durant to design the first Chevrolet automobile. Later, Louis had returned to designing race cars, but never really made any money at it. Just a few months after his victory at Indianapolis, Gaston was killed in a racing accident in Los Angeles.

Studebaker Ceases Production Of Horse-Drawn Vehicles

The Studebaker Corporation made its last horse-drawn vehicle this year. They sold their remaining stock, and parts, and machinery to a Louisville firm which continued to supply what limited market still remained of that industry. Studebaker was now only in the automobile business. None of the original founders, the five Studebaker brothers, were still living.

Henry Ford Causes His Own Dealers Much Anxiety

Henry Ford had exhausted most of his cash in paying off the Dodge brothers' law suit, plus buying out the remaining stock holders, including the Dodge brothers and James Couzens. 1920 was a depression year, despite what the super-rich bankers had promised the public would never happen again, when their Federal Reserve bill was before Congress in 1913. Cars were not selling well.

Ford lowered prices to the bone, stopped buying raw materials, and from the inventories on hand, built out all the cars he could. His dealers were forced to accept, and pay cash for, all the new cars upon delivery to the dealership; this was part of their dealer franchise agreement. If a dealer objected, he was reminded that a Ford dealership franchise was the most profitable, and therefore the most desirable franchise in all the world; that someone else would like to have that particular location; and what a shame it would be for the Ford Motor Co. to cancel the franchise agreement for such a relatively minor violation of the agreement, as not accepting a shipment of new cars.

Because of the threat of immediate cancellation, most of the over 15,000 dealers knuckled under and found ways to beg, borrow, or somehow come up with the money to buy all the Model "T" Fords that were being sent to them. Bear in mind that the Ford Motor Co., and every other car manufacturer, only has a relatively few customers, their dealers. It is the dealer who sells the cars to the public and, as soon as the dealer buys the cars from the manufacturer, they belong to the dealer, to use or dispose of as he sees fit. Henry Ford's ruthless strategy worked, and the Ford Motor Co. was able to weather this storm because of Henry Ford's personal arrogance.

1921

The Dodge Brothers Company Continues Without Its Founders

With the death of Horace Dodge in December, 1920, the estate had the former vice president and general manager, Fred Haynes, assume the presidency of the Dodge Brothers Motor Car Co.

Woodrow Wilson Buys A Used Car

When he retired from the Presidency in 1921 to make room for Warren G. Harding, Woodrow Wilson bought one of the official White House cars for his personal use. It was one of the Pierce-Arrow limousines. He became the first, and only United States President to buy a *USED* car upon leaving office. The car is now one of his personal items on display at his library in Virginia.

Durant Starts Another Auto Company

Within a month and a half after his departure from General Motors, William C. Durant went through the motions of attempting to start a new automobile company. He had done the same thing ten years earlier in 1911, when he was removed from G.M. the first time. He now named a car company after himself, for the first time. His idea of raising money was for individuals to pay for their stock in the company on the installment plan. He was able to produce the "Durant Four" car for around $900.00 by late summer. There was still a little magic in the Durant name, and soon over $30 million worth of "Durant Fours" were ordered. Then, in late 1921, he announced plans to try to compete with the Model "T" Ford by planning the "Star" auto for $350.00.

Chrysler Goes From Willys To Maxwell-Chalmers

Walter P. Chrysler did what he could to save Willys-Overland. It was almost too late when he took over, but he managed to introduce enough of his cost cutting ideas to keep the firm afloat. Meanwhile, sales of Chalmers cars and of Maxwell cars both dropped. Both vehicles were still being made in the Chalmers factory, but they were still independent companies.

Chalmers was just not that outstanding a car in the over saturated medium-price market to sell in large enough quantities to make a good profit. The Maxwell had some mechanical problems with the rear axle and gas tank mountings which, until the flaws were re-designed, caused sales to slump. Maxwell actually terminated the lease with Chalmers to manufacture their cars because Maxwell had so many un-sold cars. This caused Chalmers to go into receivership and Maxwell was able to buy the Chalmers Company for less than two million dollars. That would have been fine if Maxwell were not already over $25 million in debt.

The Maxwell-Chalmers' creditors came to Chrysler; he explained that he was under contract to Willys-Overland. The Maxwell-Chalmers creditors then went to the Willys-Overland creditors and reached an agreement to share the Chrysler talents and abilities until the Willys-Overland contract with him expired. Chrysler worked a different pay plan with Maxwell-Chalmers, however. Instead of a straight salary, he took considerably less salary, but demanded big stock options. Chrysler got himself put in charge of a committee to reorganize Maxwell-Chalmers. The company had to go up for auction, and the committee bought it back for just under $11 million. The new company had Walter P. Chrysler as Chairman of the Board of Directors.

The Lincoln Motor Co. Is Unjustly Taxed Into Receivership

The Leland-built Lincoln car made its appearance this year. It was an engineering masterpiece for its day; but, in looks, it was too boxy and too "Plain Jane" to be attractive. The result was that it didn't sell well. The United States government did more to put Lincoln into receivership than anyone else. They tried to collect four and a half million dollars taxes from the profits of the Liberty engine manufacturer. The bill for the taxes should have been for only half a million dollars, but by the time the error was corrected, the damage was done and the Lincoln Motor Car Company was in receivership.

1922

Henry Ford Gets Rid Of Henry Leland

At the urging of his wife and son to "save the Leland's", Henry Ford stepped in. The court set the price at eight million dollars. Henry Ford said that he would pay the Lincoln debts and the Lincoln stockholders, and keep 76 year old Henry Leland, and his son Wilfred, in charge. "Said" is the correct word here as all Henry Ford did was to pay the Lincoln Motor Co. debts. He soon had one of his "yes men" tell the Leland's to remove their personal belongings from the premises as their services were no longer required by Ford.

There was nothing in writing, and it was Henry Ford's word against Henry Leland's. Henry Ford's life was filled with ruthless and arrogant dealings and tactics; and Henry Leland's life was always based on honesty and fair dealings and ethical, Christian principles, so it is up to the reader to decide which Henry he chooses to believe.

The Ford engineers examined the Lincoln and could find no way to improve on the basic design of the mechanical parts; however, they did make some changes in the cooling system. They also bought a few custom bodies and adapted them to mass production to improve the Lincoln styling and appearance.

Chrysler Gets The Maxwell Flaws Corrected

While finishing his contract at Willys-Overland, Chrysler had the Maxwell short comings re-designed and eliminated, and advertised the car as the "Good" Maxwell. He cut the price of the Maxwell to only $5.00 per car profit, in order to sell the big inventory on hand. This, at least, prevented huge Maxwell losses. He also continued the Chalmers car almost exactly the way it was. Then, Chrysler obtained another fifteen million dollar loan, and had design work started on the car that would eventually be named "Chrysler".

Durant Motors Names A Car In Honor Of Flint, Michigan

In the summer, William C. Durant announced that the first six-cylinder car to be produced by his company would be the "Flint" because it would be made in Flint, Michigan where Durant had spent many of his early years.

One Of Charles Kettering's Few Mistakes

Charles F. Kettering was now a full-time employee of General Motors, since merging his DELCO company with them. He was working on an idea of his which was called the "Copper-Cooled" engine. His idea was that instead of using water and a radiator to keep the engine cool, he would weld copper fins onto the engine cylinder itself, which would dissipate heat and keep the cylinders, valves, pistons, etc., cool.

Kettering had developed sort of a way of welding copper fins to the cast iron cylinders, but it was poor at best. They got the set-up to work, "more or less", in the lab. They even made a few experimental six-cylinder "copper-cooled" engines and installed them in a few Oakland chassis for experimental purposes. The result was a disaster, because the rear cylinders did not get enough air at the right temperature to keep them cool enough. Then there was a severe

Source: *National Auto History Collection
of the Detroit Public Library*

**The Fords and the Lelands at the
Transfer of Lincoln Ownership (inside)**

The transfer of the Lincoln Motor Co. ownership from Henry M. Leland to Henry Ford, February 19, 1922. The indoor photo shows left to right: Henry M. Leland, Mr. & Mrs. Edsel Ford, Mr. & Mrs. Henry Ford, Mr. & Mrs. Wilfred Leland.

The Fords and the Lelands at the Transfer of Lincoln Ownership (outside)

The Lincoln Motor Company Changes Hands

The outdoor photo, with the Lincoln Motor Co. main entrance as the background shows, from left to right: Henry M. Leland, Mr. and Mrs. Wilfred Leland, Mr. & Mrs. Edsel Ford, Mr. & Mrs. Henry Ford.

Source: *National Auto History Collection of the Detroit Public Library*

Flint Display At An Automobile Show

Source: *National Auto History Collection
of the Detroit Public Library*

**Mr. Beniamiano Gigli, Tenor,
Metropolitan Opera Star, About To Enter His New Flint Touring Car.**

1924-25 Flint

The Flint was built as a competitor to cars in the Buick size and price range by Durant Motors. As were all cars built by Durant Motors, it was an "assembled" car. Because of Durant Motor's questionable financial condition, the Flint was only made for a couple of years. It was named for the city of Flint, Michgan, where Mr. Durant had spent many of his early years and of which he had many fond memories.

detonation knock, or ping, even at normal temperatures, plus a few other problems.

Kettering got the set-up to work somewhat better in the four-cylinder engine, so Chevrolet made 500 of them and installed them in late 1922 into 1923 model cars. Most, if not all, were used by Chevrolet Motor Co. representatives, and people in that capacity, just as experimental cars. There were so bad that all were called back and had regular engines and radiators installed, and the experiment was abandoned. Henry Ford bought one to study; they still have it in the Ford museum to this day.

On the positive side of Kettering's abilities, 1922 was the year when he perfected the anti-knock gasoline formula he had been striving for. By adding tetra-ethyl lead, the engine would not "ping". Tetra-ethyl lead was shortened to "ethyl" and is the same substance environmentalists are now saying pollutes air.

1923

Mr. Chrysler Finalizes Details To Bring Out The "Chrysler" Car

Walter P. Chrysler was still making all the pieces fit together in order to bring out a car with his name on it; he was exercising his stock options to buy all the Maxwell-Chalmers stock he could. He continued making the Maxwell but began to phase out the Chalmers. His engineers were building some pilot models of his new and "completely different" car, which was to have the name Chrysler. He needed about five million dollars to get it into actual production, but his banker friends declined to loan that kind of money on an un-tested car. There were already over one hundred brands of cars being made in 1923 in this country, and only a very few were successful enough to warrant that high a loan.

November was the time for the automobile show in New York City to introduce the new models for the next year. He was told that he could not exhibit his Chryler cars, as they were pilot models, and the show was for cars that were actually in production and ready for a person to buy. Maxwell and Chalmers were production cars so they could be shown. Chrysler knew that all the automobile executives stayed at the Hotel Commodore, so he rented the Commodore lobby and displayed his pilot models there. Several hundred orders were taken for the pilot model Chrysler's which was enough to convince the bankers to go ahead and loan Chrysler the extra five million needed to get the cars into production.

Packard Starts A Trend With Their Straight Eight Engine

Packard was far and away the undisputed prestige car of the time. It was the ultimate car everyone wanted to own and to be seen in. With the economic slump of 1920 and 1921, Packard decided to have an engine type to give more power, and speed, and economy. In 1923, they introduced their straight 8 engine which consisted of eight cylinders in a line, one behind the other. Packard still kept producing a six for their lower-priced cars, and temporarily kept the twin six V-12 for another year.

During the next ten years every other car maker in the country who built high or medium-priced cars, would either have a straight 8, or have experimented with it, or considered it. Packard was not the first to have a straight 8. Dusenberg already had one, but it

1925 Pierce-Arrow

Pierce-Arrow was still using its excellent, but slow and out-dated six cylinder engine in 1925. Its chief competitors all had eight-cylinder engines, Lincoln and Cadillac with V-8's and Packard with a straight eight. By the time Pierce-Arrow brought out an eight-cylinder engine, it was too late. The die had been cast.

1926 Pierce-Arrow Touring Car   1925 Pierce-Arrow Roadster

Both vehicles are Pierce-Arrow. They were available with standard headlights, but most people chose the distinctive fender mounted type as this was a Pierce-Arrow exclusive which no other car maker ever attempted to imitate.

166

took the resources behind the Packard name to make it engineered right, and to make it popular.

What The Term "Assembled Car" Means

While this chronicle deals primarily with cars whose names are still household words, it is appropriate to mention the "assembled car". These "assembled car" companies were in their hey-day in the 1920's; they consisted of one or more people assembling their own car from parts which were made by other well known, specialty companies. Engines would be bought from an independent engine manufacturer; transmissions from a transmission manufacturer; likewise for radiators, axles, frames, bodies, wheels, steering parts, and all of the component parts. A quantity of each of the component parts would be bought and delivered to one location, where they were all assembled into a finished automobile. In some cases, the assemblers would build one of the components themselves, usually the bodies, or fenders and hoods, and buy all the mechanical parts from other suppliers.

There were over one hundred different brands of cars made in this country in 1923, over sixty-five of which were "assembled" cars. Some brands even made more than one model, using different engines from different makers for different models. There were about ten engine makers who supplied the "assembled" car producers. Continental (Red Seal) was the most popular engine maker; Herschell-Spillman was also a major supplier of engines, as was Buda. The idea of "assembled" cars was doomed, because the "assembled" car companies could not make a car of equal quality for a price as competitive as the large auto manufacturer could, where costs could be more accurately controlled; nor did the "assembled" car producers have the necessary money for much advertising. They could not attract an excellent dealer organization, because the good dealers would be more likely to go with or stay with a well-known, established company. The assembled car producers had little to offer a dealer or customer in the way of technical assistance, other than to refer them to the manufacturer of the particular component that was causing the problem.

The main attraction which "assembled" car producers had was that most people who bought from them were buying their first car, and didn't want a Ford, or were skeptical of the big companies that were already so rich.

The idea of an "assembled" car was not new. As a matter of fact, the Buick Motor Co. of 1902-1903, in Detroit, was just that, a manufacturer of motors (engines) for other fledgling automobile and boat producers of the time. It wasn't until 1904, after it had moved to Flint, that more than a dozen cars were made by Buick.

Durant's Car Companies Pass Their Peak In Popularity

The new Durant Motors Co. was made up entirely of "assembled" cars. This year was the turning point for Durant Motors, primarily because Mr. Durant presumed that there was magic in his name and that people would automatically buy whatever he was associated with. The same reason that Durant Motors was failing now was exactly the same reason for which Mr. Durant had brought General Motors down twice in ten years. Durant was more interested in the stock market than he was in making cars. As long as he was making money in the stock market, he took almost no interest in Durant Motors.

During the 1920's, it was quite easy for an experienced speculator, such as William C. Durant, to make money on Wall Street. Back in 1902 and 1903, he had been in New York so much of the time playing the stock market that he seriously considered resigning from the Durant-Dort Carriage Company; this was before Durant had ever even heard of Buick. The

THE Moon car is designed to appeal to people who are distinguished from the masses by higher ideals—not necessarily by larger bank accounts.

It meets their requirements in looks, comfort and service. Its superb coachwork—exclusive upholstery and grace of design lend charm and beauty to its reliable mechanical construction.

MOON CARS

A few Moon features

Red Seal Continental motors—Rayfield carburetors—long wheel base—Delco starting, lighting and igniting—one-man top—extra long springs—complete chassis and body equipment.

The Moon Sixes

Six-43—5-Passenger Touring Car—$1395
Six-45—4-Passenger *Club* Roadster—$1485
Six-66—7-Passenger Touring Car—4-Passenger *Club* Roadster—$1750

MOON MOTOR CAR CO.,   ST. LOUIS, U. S. A.

Prices subject to advance without notice.

This MOON touring car of 1917 is a typical example of an "assembled" car. Continental engines were featured in several makes of "assembled" cars.

CONNECTICUT IGNITION

Full Current—and What It Means To Gasoline

THE Connecticut System is free to deliver the battery's full current to your cylinders because no resistance has been set up anywhere along the line to cut down the flow.

Full current means a fat, eager spark which fires rapidly and completely even today's low-grade fuels.

That fat spark is necessary to get the maximum miles per gallon from your gasoline. With gasoline at 35 cents full current will prevent high fuel bills.

The Automatic Switch guarantees the system's safety in using full current —because when the motor stops the current stops—the switch kicks off automatically and checks the flow.

Will the Connecticut Ignition System be on the next car you buy?

CONNECTICUT TELEPHONE & ELECTRIC **COMPANY**
Meriden   Connecticut

One of the suppliers of electrical components to "assembled car" builders in 1920. Note the price of gasoline at .35¢ a gallon!

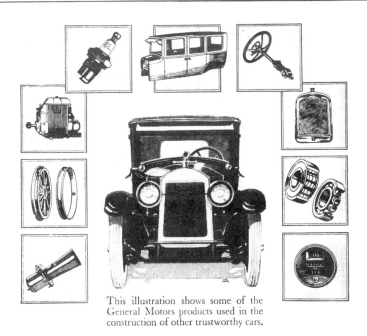

This illustration shows some of the General Motors products used in the construction of other trustworthy cars.

Contributing to the merit of many trustworthy cars

Within the General Motors family are a score of companies producing parts, accessories and equipment.

Much of their output is sold to other automobile manufacturers here and abroad; while some of the products of the accessory divisions find a wide variety of uses outside the automotive industry.

Thus General Motors contributes to the merit of many other trustworthy cars and to almost every phase of home and industrial life.

GENERAL MOTORS

BUICK · CADILLAC · CHEVROLET · OAKLAND
OLDSMOBILE · GMC TRUCKS

This 1925 ad shows that General Motors contributed to the "assembled car" trend in the 1920's. General Motors had nothing to lose as long as the assembled car maker could pay for their parts.

Source: *National Auto History Collection
of the Detroit Public Library*

Formal Photo Of William C. Durant Taken In 1926

All Models Equipped with Disc Steel Wheels and Cord Tires

Chalmers Motor Car Company, Detroit, Michigan

Chalmers Motor Company of Canada, Limited, Windsor, Ontario

The
CHALMERS
SIX

The Chalmers was part of the Maxwell-Chalmers group that Mr. Chrysler used to bring out a car with his name. When this ad appeared in 1922, the end of the Chalmers name was very near.

Source: *National Auto History Collection
of the Detroit Public Library*

One of the last Chalmers sedans was this 1923 model. A very few were made for 1924.

Buick stockholders had to wait for him to come back to Flint from New York City in 1904, to talk to him about getting into Buick.

After its initial two-year flash-in-the-pan, which was now past, Durant Motors proceded progressively down hill into eventual oblivion.

Henry Ford's Power Is At Its Peak

The year of 1923 was when Henry Ford was at his peak in popularity. Never again would he be so highly respected personally; never again would his car be so successful. His dealings in the past with those who knew him when he was poor were not extensively reported to the general public, and the general public did not want to believe the few unpleasant things they had heard or read. Just over two million Model "T" Fords were built, the highest production of any one year.

Cadillac Establishes The Flat Rate Labor System

This was the year when General Motors had Cadillac inaugurate a policy which has turned into a boon for the company, and which has been copied by the other car makers of today. The policy was the establishment of a flat rate for the time, converted to dollars and cents, that certain specified repairs should take. One of the reasons for this flat rate system is so that a customer will know how much the labor should cost before agreeing to it.

1924

Buick Imitates, But Only "Packard Can Build A Packard"

This is the year when Buick paid Packard just about the most sincere compliment it could pay, by making the Buick hood and radiator look like the Packard hood and radiator. Several cars of the era had very distinctive looking frontal appearances; the Pierce-Arrow, with its lights in the fenders was at one end of the scale; and the Model "T" Ford, where the wheels stuck out in front further than anything else, was at the other end of the scale. Why did Buick pick Packard to copy? Because a Packard had a reputation and distinction greater than any other car! Besides Buick, Willys-Knight also imitated the Packard look. Packard's reply was to keep the Packard unchanged, as was its practice, and its advertisment: "Only Packard Can Build A Packard".

The Quiet Stanley Scoops The Others With "Juice" Brakes

This was also the year when one of the best known names of the time came out with something on their cars that every other make eventually copied, hydraulic four-wheel brakes. Many people are under the false impression that all Chrysler cars always had hydraulic four-wheel brakes, but this is not the case. The manufacturer who installed them on all its cars, starting with the 1924 models was Stanley Steamer. Stanley's cars were quite

A "Shabby" Car In The 1920's

Typical street scene in the late 1920's. It seems ironic that the Model "T" Ford shown here should be parked in front of the second hand store. The condition of this car would have been described during the 1920's as a "shabby". It is dirty, the top is stretched and baggy, a spare tire is hanging over the dummy left front door which does not open. The side curtains make the whole overall scene look that much dirtier.

When a new Model "T" Ford touring car could be bought for around $300.00 during this era, an older one, in this condition, would probably sell for $25.00, providing it was in running order.

ONLY
PACKARD
CAN BUILD A
PACKARD

Willys-Knight was one of the imitators of the Packard radiator and hood style. Buick also featured this style for several years during the mid 1920's. Packard's reply was to remind everyone that "Only Packard Can Build A Packard". The Packard is the upper illustration here and the lower one is Willys-Knight.

fast and powerful, and their brakes now approached being adequate.

When Mr. Chrysler introduced cars with his name on them, he built enough Chalmers cars to finish using the remaining component parts. For this year and the next, the Maxwell name was still being used. During 1925 Chrysler's name was put on what was formerly known as the Maxwell, but the engine, and chassis, and two-wheel mechanical brakes were not basically changed. The advertising for the "Chrysler Four" mentioned that hydraulic four-wheel brakes were "available at slight extra cost".

Kettering Shows His Genius In Selling "Duco"

Charles F. Kettering, the genius of General Motors, has countless inventions to his credit, to more than offset the mistake of the copper-cooled engine. He was responsible for something else taking place to greatly speed up automobile production, although he was not directly responsible for the invention itself. That was the method of painting a car.

Until the early 1920's, painting a car body was probably the slowest part of production and its biggest bottle-neck. The finish had to be brushed on by hand, then allowed to dry, sanded to get the brush marks out, painted again, with the entire process repeated until three or four coats of primer and finish, usually varnish, were applied; then the body was ready to be installed on the chassis. This body painting process usually took about a month. Small parts could be spray-painted, but black was the only color which turned out to be acceptable.

On July 4, 1920, a chemist had been working overtime at DuPont when he hit upon the solution. He called it "nitrocellulose lacquer". It took some time to conduct the necessary experiments to make sure it would hold up under all kinds of weather, and be available in a rainbow of colors. The DuPont chemists also had to arrive at just the right thickness of the liquid paint, and had to get the right spray equipment to apply it smoothly.

Then came one of the hardest things DuPont had to do, and that was selling the automobile manufacturers the idea of using the new paint. The automobile manufacturers willingly accepted the new paint because it speeded up new car production so much, and also because it made so many new, fresh colors available. The paint manufacturers, however, were not really very enthusiastic about the new paint, because it meant re-training so many employees in a different method of mixing and a new method of spraying. The new paint also meant junking much varnish making equipment, plus the training of workers in repair shops all across the country on how to use the new paint and on how to spray it properly.

Kettering dramatized the situation in a very unusual,and yet successful way. He invited a big executive of one of the large paint companies to come to his office and be prepared to spend the day. As soon as the executive arrived, Kettering showed him some samples of different colored paints and asked him which he would choose for his next car, if all those colors were available. The paint executive indicated his choice, and they went on with their visit. Kettering and the paint executive talked paint, talked cars, swapped yarns, and had lunch in the company cafeteria inside the company plant. They generally got to know each other quite well, and had a nice, friendly visit.

Finally, around 4:30 P.M., or so, the paint executive said he would have to be leaving, as he had to take care of some other matters. Kettering then walked him out to the parking lot to his car. When they arrived near the spot, Kettering asked where he had parked, whereupon the paint executive replied that the car in the space did not look like his, although it was the same make and model. When they walked up to the car, the paint executive realized what Kettering had done. He had his workers take the man's car and paint it the color of his choice within just a matter of hours, instead of the long drawn out process it used to take.

This dramatization convinced the paint executive that he should go ahead, change over

CHRYSLER FOUR—*Touring Car*, $895; *Club Coupe*, $995; *Coach*, $1045; *Sedan*, $1095. *Hydraulic four-wheel brakes at slight extra cost.*
CHRYSLER SIX—*Phaeton*, $1395; *Coach*, $1445; *Roadster*, $1625; *Sedan*, $1695; *Royal Coupe*, $1795; *Brougham*, $1865; *Imperial*, $1995; *Crown Imperial*, $2095.
All prices f. o. b. Detroit, subject to current Federal excise tax.
Bodies by Fisher on all Chrysler enclosed models. All models equipped with full balloon tires.

Many people think that all Chrysler cars always had hydraulic four wheel brakes. This ad shows that they were considered an accessory on the lowest priced model.

This ad also refers to the Fisher body on the enclosed cars. Fisher built bodies for many auto makers during the 1920's, including the Essex. Fisher was not a General Motors subsidiary at the time.

Source: *National Auto History Collection
of the Detroit Public Library*

Kettering In The Lab

Charles F. Kettering is in action in the laboratory. He was completely at home in the lab, always testing one idea or another, always looking to improve.

Just two years after its initial acceptance, in 1924, by Oakland of General Motors, DUCO became widely used by a large number of U.S. and foreign auto makers. This ad appeared in 1926

their manufacturing equipment, and re-train the company workers. The name of the new paint was taken from the first syllable of each word of the *DuPont Company* name, which was DUCO; and the paint still has that name. The first mass produced car to use DUCO as the factory finish, was the 1924 Oakland. Within two years, competitors of DUCO were also available, and virtually every car manufacturer was using the process.

1925

Australian Brothers Use G.M. Cars Across Syrian Desert

A delightful adventure story was taking place in the mid 1920's and, while not directly a part of Cadillac history, the venture would probably have not taken place the way it did had there been no Cadillac car.

After World War I ended, two Australian brothers elected to be discharged from the British Army in the middle east, where they had both served during the war. For a while, they bought and sold surplus government vehicles for a little profit. Then, using some of these vehicles, they began hauling passengers up and down the Mediterranean coast, between Beirut and Haifa, along with what ever freight they could manage to strap to the fenders and running boards.

The French had been assigned authority as protectorate of Syria on the Mediterranean, and the British as protectorate of Iraq. Since oil had recently been discovered in Iraq, many British people were there on business from time to time, but when it came time for them to go back to England, it took almost a month by ship. The British thought it would be jolly good if the brothers would open a car route from Beirut to Bagdad, some 600 miles away.

Of course, no one had yet established a regular modern travel route of any kind for large scale service, although a couple of expeditions had crossed the desert by car during World War I at considerable expense for machinery. Air travel was just as hot as automobile travel, and each method averaged about 60 miles an hour, but air travel was terribly expensive. A railroad was out of the question because it would be too expensive to build and maintain.

There was known to be a tribe of wandering nomads, called the Bedouins, who were described as notorious thieves, roaming the desolate area of the desert route, and, who, threatening with knives or guns, took whatever they wanted, whenever and wherever they wanted it, along the desert route. A smuggler was reported to have hauled his desert wares along the desert route by camel caravan, paying off the Bedouins not to bother his caravans. For the equivalent of 2,000 British Pounds a year, this smuggler guaranteed the safe passage of cars following the route through the desert.

The British and French both let the Australian brothers have lucrative mail contracts to help sweeten the pot a little and encourage establishment of the car caravan on a regular schedule.

In dry weather, most of the desert was hard surface, although there was a stretch of about fifty miles of softer sand. During World War I and afterward, the two Australian brothers discovered the good and bad points of cars built around the world. For a car caravan across the desert on a regular schedule, they considered Cadillac the best car, although they also had some Buicks. Since there were no places to stop for food, or fuel, or water, or other

FACTS ABOUT A FAMOUS FAMILY

Part of a convoy of General Motors cars en route from Beirut to Bagdad. Speed as high as 70 miles an hour is attained during the 600 mile trip.

Beirut to Bagdad

It used to take about four weeks to travel from London to Bagdad. To-day, through the service of General Motors cars, you can make the trip in *eight days*.

Across the Syrian Desert—between Beirut on the Mediterranean and Bagdad in Persia — convoys of Buicks and Cadillacs are carrying passengers and mails on a regular schedule. Though heavily laden, they cover 600 miles of sandy waste in less than 24 hours of running—most of the trip at racing speed.

The stamina of General Motors cars and trucks has led to their selection wherever the going is hardest. You will find them in every country of the world.

GENERAL MOTORS

BUICK · CADILLAC · CHEVROLET · OAKLAND
OLDSMOBILE · GMC TRUCKS

General Motors trucks and Delco-Light products may be purchased on the *GMAC* Payment Plan. Insurance service furnished by General Exchange Corporation.

supplies, everything had to be carried on board the cars themselves. Usually, about six cars would travel together, sometimes as many as a dozen. They never went alone.

Since the desert surface was so hard, except for that one stretch of less than fifty miles, and since there was no other traffic around, the cars would usually be run wide open, at around 70 miles an hour. The caravan would start out in late afternoon and drive all night, when it was cooler and therefore easier on the passengers, the cars, and the tires. When there was rain and the hard desert was slippery, the surface was like ice.

If an animal were to run out in front of a car, and if the driver swerved to try to avoid it, the car would likely spin around several times, or go sideways for a while with usually no damage, but the passengers would be supplied with quite a story to tell for the rest of their lives. On occasion, some Arabs would try to rob a caravan of cars; they would have to attempt a robbery from ambush, as the cars could outrun the Arabian horses after the horses got winded. The schedules were maintained, so the Arabs knew when to expect them.

From time to time, the various political situations would become uncertain, and another route, usually longer, would have to be taken, at least until things settled back down. Countless stories are told about things that happened on these trips, such as mirages and sand storms; cars being shot up and having to be left on the desert to be retrieved several days later; back seat passengers occasionally bumped their noses on the wooden top bow of the touring car, when thrown up off the seat as the car went over a bad bump, and drivers having to wear gloves to change a flat tire that was so hot that it would catch on fire. So many stories were told, it might be hard to tell fact from fiction, but they were probably all based on fact.

Eventually, the route was extended beyond Bagdad to Teheran, Persia. Drivers for these cars would have to have been quite adventuresome. They were a wild living group, except when it came to their passengers' comfort and well being, which always came first. Eventually, in the 1930's, as roads were built, the old touring cars were replaced by busses. Some of these venerable old Cadillacs and Buicks reportedly had close to a quarter of a million miles on them when they were retired from service.

Henry Ford's Refusal To Change Lets Chevrolet Get Ahead

This was the first year when more Chevrolets were made than Model "T" Fords. Chevrolet, now making only one model, was at the right place at the right time and owed its success to three major factors: the popularity of the enclosed car, the refusal of Henry Ford to bring his car up to date, and Chevrolet's learning experience from Ford's mistakes. Ever since the popularity of the low-priced Essex sedan was evidenced in the car market, the other low-priced car makers did what Hudson had done with the Essex, that is to make a crackerbox shaped enclosed car, with low-priced cloth upholstery and fittings.

Ford went through the motions of doing this with the Model "T" but that was Ford's big mistake. The Model "T" engine and chassis were designed for the lighter weight of an open car, and since enclosed bodies were considerably heavier, the Model "T" was just not up to the task of moving it around. This is what Chevrolet learned from Ford's mistake.

Chevrolet had come out with two improved and redesigned chassis since 1919, when the Essex was introduced. Each had a four-cylinder engine and was considered to be a light chassis, but each was an improvement over the one before it. Ford's basic chassis had not been changed since 1909.

Another idea Ford refused to accept was that the enclosed car was not a passing fad. 1925 was the year when the enclosed car production equalled open car production in this country for the first time. Chevrolet's production facilities were no greater than Ford's, but Chevrolet had kept up with the times and made the kind of a car the public would go into debt to buy for

Source: *National Auto History Collection
of the Detroit Public Library*

1925-1926 Chevrolet "Superior" Touring Car

Chevrolet "490" Chassis of the Late Teens and Early 1920's

Some quite obvious differences exist between the 490 series and the Superior series Chevrolet. The shorter springs and the exposed engine valve mechanism are the 490. The more modern Superior chassis has the longer frame and springs, and enclosed engine valves.

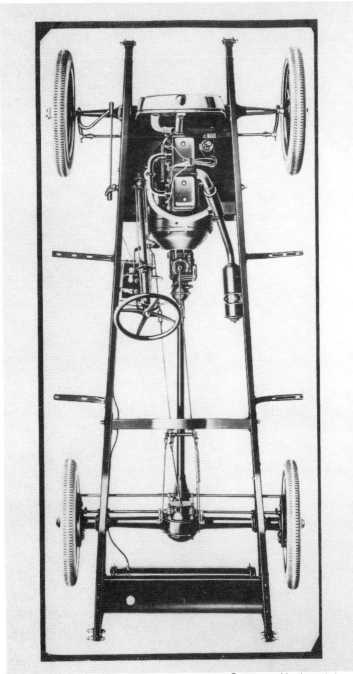

Source: *National Auto History Collection*
of the Detroit Public Library

Chevrolet "Superior" Chassis of 1925-26

This Chevrolet Superior was the final blow to the Model "T" Ford because it was a much better value. It cost a little more, but people were willing to pay a little more for the Chevrolet. It had a much more modern chassis than the Model "T" Ford which had not basically changed for 15 years since 1909. The later 1925-26 Superior, shown here, was improved over the earlier Superior.

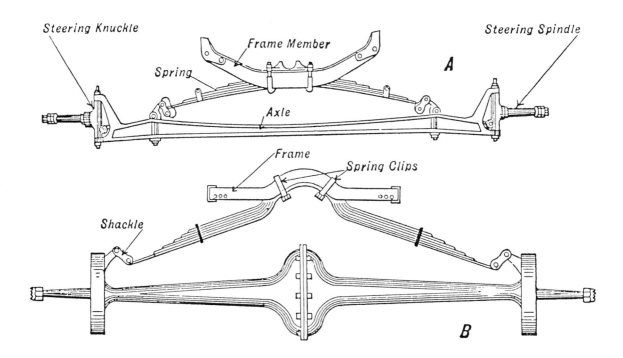

Ford Spring Suspension

The type used by Ford was known as transverse, which means that the spring was parallel to the axle, perpendicular to the wheels. Most other cars had two springs per axle, the springs being parallel to the wheels. As can be seen in these illustrations, the transverse springs are attached to the frame of the car only at the center; this allowed more sway and leaning than the other type. The top drawing is the front axle. Ford kept this same basic design as long as Henry Ford was alive and did not modernize until the 1949 models were introduced.

The Model A Ford (1928-1931) had each spring slightly longer. During the 1930's and 1940's the springs were lengthened a little more, then had brackets (shackles) attached to the axles to lower the height of the car's body. The basic design remained unchanged on all Fords, Mercurys, Lincoln Zephyrs, and Lincoln Continentals through the 1948 models.

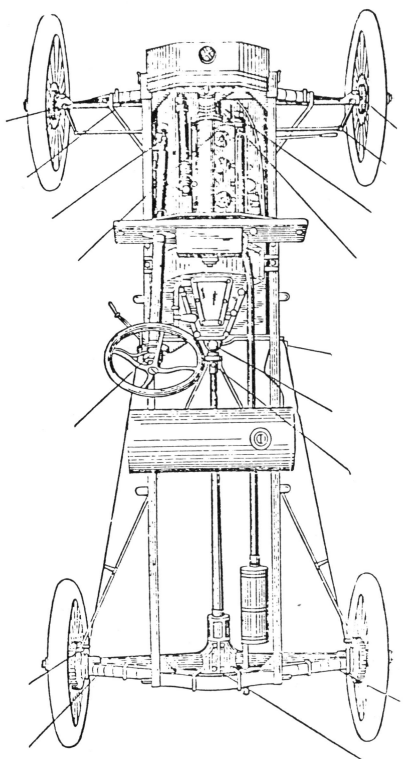

Overhead View Of The Model "T" Ford Chassis

The one shown is a 1914-1915-1916 with the brass radiator. The basic design remained the same from 1909 through 1927, with only extremely minor changes.

188

Commonwealth Chevrolet Co.

Source: *National Auto History Collection
of the Detroit Public Library*

1929 Chevrolets In Dealer Showroom

The main emphasis of this photo is on the chassis which has several parts chrome plated and others "cut away" to show the internal mechanical workings. This was the first Chevrolet to have a six-cylinder engine. Both Ford and Chevrolet had introduced four-wheel brakes one model year earlier.

The chassis was not equipped with shock absorbers, which were accessories in 1929. On the far left, with the front half almost completely hidden by the coach and the potted fern on the table, is a peddler's truck on the half ton chassis, almost identical to the passenger car chassis.

SIX-SIXTY-SIX

$**895**

and upwards
all prices at factory
LANSING, MICH.
112 in. WHEELBASE

DURANT MOTORS, INC., DETROIT, U.S.A.
DURANT MOTOR COMPANY OF CALIFORNIA,
OAKLAND, CALIFORNIA
DURANT MOTORS OF CANADA, LTD., LEASIDE, ONT.

SIX-SEVENTY

$**1195**

and upwards
all prices at factory
LANSING, MICH.
119 IN. WHEELBASE

The Six-Seventy De Luxe Sedan, $1425

D U R A N T
A   G O O D   C A R

Durant Motors was almost out of business when this ad appeared in 1929. Mr. Durant made one last attempt to save his name by hiring some of the former Dodge Brothers' executives, displaced when Mr. Chrysler bought Dodge; but it was too late. Mr. Durant's methods were destined to fail again as they had done in the past.

Source: *National Auto History Collection
of the Detroit Public Library*

1929 Chevrolet Landau Sedan

Source: *National Auto History Collection
of the Detroit Public Library*

1929 Ford And 1929 Chevrolet Compared

1929 Chevrolet with disc wheels and landau irons and the 1929 Ford Model "A" tudor (the way Ford spelled TWO DOOR) with wire wheels and an accessory quail on the radiator cap.

Chevrolet came out with a six-cylinder engine for 1929 which cut greatly into the sales of the four-cylinder Model "A" Ford, introduced in 1928. Chevrolet did not use a strong enough rear axle for its six-cylinder engine, resulting in many broken axle shafts. It was not uncommon for a Chevrolet owner to carry an extra new axle shaft and a couple of coat hangers under the front seat, with the rest of the tools. The coat hangers were used to wrap around the broken piece of axle shaft which remained inside the axle housing in order to pull it out.

$550.00, rather than buy an open Ford roadster with a crank for under $300.00.

The Dodge Brothers' Estates Sell To Bankers

The estate of the two Dodge brothers decided to sell the company. Everyone had been watching the company's progress since John and Horace had both died in 1920. To the surprise of all concerned, the company was growing the way it probably would have done, had the two brothers still been alive to run things.

The Dodge Brothers Motor Car Co. was sold to a banking group headed by Dillon, Read, and Co. of New York City, in July, 1925. The price was $146 million and was the largest transaction this country had ever seen until that time.

This was a turning point; it proved that you had to have a banker to succeed. Every successful automobile firm in this country was controlled by bankers, as well as several automobile firms that were not so successful. Ford was no longer one of the successful companies; its production was dropping steadily, and high production was absolutely essential in building the cheapest kind of product. Ford was still in the business of making large quantities of very cheap cars; cheap in price, and cheap in quality, as compared to other new cars available at the time.

The parade had now passed by Henry Ford because, as the rest of the United States automobile industry was advancing, Henry Ford insisted that his company stand perfectly still.

The Late 1920's

Original Pioneers Mostly Gone

We have covered important events that took place for a period of thirty years, concerning the automobile pioneers and their companies, whose names are still household words. We have also shown other bits and pieces of history, which affected all of us in the United States and our culture, because of the effect of the automobile business on our total economy.

In the beginning, in 1895, the individual men who were the automobile pioneers, were deeply involved in their individual companies. By 1925, however, too many cars were being made in the total U.S. production of cars for any one individual executive to continue to be personally involved. A few of the early pioneers had died, some had retired, and some had left the automobile business for other fields. Henry Ford was the only one of the original pioneers who, as an individual, was still active with his original company in 1925.

Charles W. Nash was active in 1925, but he was not one of the really old time pioneers, since he did not come into the automobile business until 1906, and then as a Buick production foreman. Walter P. Chrysler was also still active in 1925, but neither did he come into the automobile business until 1911, and, then also as a Buick production foreman, succeeding Nash.

Charles F. Kettering was active in 1925, but a car was never named for him, and his name is no longer a household word.

William C. Durant was no longer active in the automobile business, although a company

Source: *National Auto History Collection of the Detroit Public Library*

1925 Lincolns In Showroom

There is only one touring car on display plus two enclosed sedans, and a town car, whose top snapped over the driver's seat is barely visible. While it is not possible to tell the body style of the car nearest the camera, it only had the standard two-wheel brakes, as did the touring car here. It was possible to order a new Lincoln with four-wheel brakes, or have your present Lincoln converted to four-wheel brakes.

With its peppy V-8 engine, the Lincoln was a reasonably fast car. During these prohibition days, special Lincoln touring cars, known as "police flyers", were available to law enforcement agencies. Chicago bought several and bootleggers could seldom out run them in the city. Other police departments found them equally well-suited for catching bad guys.

That New

WILLYS·KNIGHT

Unequaled *performance* · unequaled *economy* · A new name for *smoothness* · · A new high mark for *efficiency* · · An engine you'll never wear out · · ·

Great engineers, great scientists, great inventors—prominent men in all walks of life, such as Franklin D. Roosevelt, former Assistant Secretary of the Navy; Dr. Lee de Forest, the "father" of radio; Glenn Curtiss, famous aeroplane inventor; Hiram P. Maxim, President of the Maxim Silencer Company; Bud Fisher, the noted cartoonist—are outspoken in their enthusiasm over the wonderful smoothness of the new Willys-Knight.

In addition to the vast fundamental advantages of the Willys-Knight sleeve-valve engine over poppet-valve engines—there is built into this marvelous engine a great English invention that *prevents* engine vibration at any speed—the celebrated Lanchester Balancer. Willys-Knight is the only car in the United States equipped with this great advance in engineering.

Automobile engineers have yet to invent and build another type of engine that possesses

the long-wearing qualities of the Willys-Knight engine. Fifty thousand miles of uninterrupted service is commonplace, the usual thing, with this extraordinary engine. And even after five, six, seven years or more, when other engines have spent their life, the Willys-Knight engine is still young. Repair costs are next to nothing. For this engine has no clashing cams, no hammering push-rods, no pounding valves—no carbon troubles—no valve-grinding. It's an engine you'll *never wear out!*

Hand in hand with this progressive engineering is coupled a marked progress in coach-building. It is only natural that such a car should also excel in luxury. See it—drive it—and it's a hundred to one you will want it more than you have ever wanted a car before.

WILLYS-OVERLAND, INC., Toledo, Ohio
Willys-Overland Sales Co. Limited, Toronto, Canada

WILLYS · OVERLAND · FINE · MOTOR · CARS

with his name on it was producing cars in 1925. The business affairs of this company, however, were actually run by others, while Durant's individual attention was occupied with affairs of the stock market.

A Future President Endorses An Automobile

Due to the misfortune of his contracting polio in 1921, Franklin D. Roosevelt had considerable medical expenses and was unable to work for a couple of years. These events caused him a somewhat embarrassing cash flow problem. When he had sufficiently recovered from polio to return to gainful employment, he became financially interested in several ventures in addition to his law practice and his first love, politics.

In 1926, F. D. R. permitted his name to be used in an endorsement about the smoothness of the Willys-Knight automobile. Apparently F. D. R. historians consider the endorsement extremely insignificant in nature, or else are unaware of its existence.

The amount, or nature, of the compensation received by F. D. R. from Willys-Knight has not been determined. It is the only known incident where a future President of the United States endorsed an automobile.

In 1927, a close relative of his died and left F. D. R. over half a million dollars which he was able to invest wisely which ended his cash flow problems.

Mechanical Improvements In The 1920's

The late 1920's saw quite a few mechanical and general improvements in automobile manufacture which, along with the creature comforts of enclosed car bodies, made motoring much more pleasant, dependable, and safe. The improvements were, in particular: balloon tires; four wheel brakes, hydraulic brakes, enclosed brakes; standardizing the gearshift; no clash shifting; windshield wipers; stop lights; hydraulic shock absorbers; and the mechanical fuel pump. Many of the changes originated in the early 1920's and were constantly improved, so that by the end of the 1920's most of the design flaws were out of the picture, and mechanics knew how to repair the new designs. As with most accessories, changes originated on the more expensive cars, then were eventually adapted to the lower-priced models.

Balloon Tires

"Balloon" tires received their name due to the improvements in riding qualities which they gave a car in comparison to the type of tire they replaced. Until the advent of "balloon" tires, the main object of tires was to support the car on somewhat a cushion of air. The earlier tires usually carried 50 to 60 pounds of air pressure, depending on the size of the tire and the weight of the car. Although tires had been constantly improved as to dependability and quality down through the years, tires still remained one of the car owner's greatest single expenses. The basic design of the tires had not been changed. It was quite common for big, heavy, expensive cars to be equipped with two spare tires, mounted and ready for change when needed. The theory behind this was that one might get two flat tires on a trip of 150 to 200 miles. In addition, most drivers kept one or two extra usable inner tubes plus a hand tire pump, (if the car was not equipped with an engine driven tire pump) plus a repair kit to patch a tire and an inner tube.

Balloon tires were much wider than others, the sides were much taller, and much more flexible, and they required only 30 to 35 pounds of air pressure. At first, balloon tires were

Tire Chains

Chains were suggested for all four wheels, by the people who made them of course, in the days when tires were narrow and had no tread on the front tires. This 1920 ad shows no tread on the rear tires, either, which was not unusual at the time.

made to fit existing rims and wheels so that only the tire, itself, was different. This didn't work out too well, even though the car was much smoother riding because, with the wider tires, a broader rubber tire surface was touching the road. This made the car harder to steer, which was partly solved by installing a larger diameter steering wheel; and soon it was realized that balloon tires would also work much better with wheels with a smaller diameter. Then came the condition known as "shimmy" and "wheel tramp". This problem led to redesigning the front axle and springs so adjustments could be made to achieve proper alignment of caster, camber, and toe in. Then followed a change in the steering gear ratios so that steering became easier and required more turns from all the way right to all the way left.

Four Wheel Brakes, Hydraulic Brakes, and Enclosed Brakes

The reason car manufacturers gave for not installing brakes on the front wheels, as well as the rear, was simply that it was "unsafe". Several manufacturers, however, adopted them within a matter of a couple of years. Like balloon tires, front wheel brakes had to evolve too.

The early front wheel brakes were the same basic design as the rear brakes, that is, the brake band with lining was on the outside of the brake drum. When one stepped on the brake pedal, a series of rods and levers caused the brake band to contract, or squeeze together, on the outside of the brake drum. The wheel was bolted to the brake drum, so that when the drum revolved slower, or stopped, so did the wheel. Everything was O.K. until one went through a puddle of water. Since all of the mechanism, as well as the lining and braking surface, was exposed, they became ineffective when wet. If both brakes on the same side got soaked, while both on the other side remained dry, it was quite an adventure to try to stop the car.

For a short while, the early hydraulic brakes were these outside band type, too. The big advantage of hydraulic brakes was that the pressure applied to all the wheels was equal; also hydraulic brakes required considerably less pressure from the driver's pressing on the brake pedal than did the mechanical type. For one reason or another, the brake rods on the mechanical systems would become uneven, as one rod or cable or lever on one side of the system would become rusted and stick before the other side did. This would cause one side of the brake system to pull and have a little more wear.

Until Chrysler converted completely to four-wheel brakes, its four-cylinder cars actually had hydraulic outside brakes on the rear wheels only, or mechanically operated outside brakes on the rear wheels only, depending on the exact model-year of the particular car.

General Motors had committed itself to the outside band brakes for the rear wheels by having the parts either on hand, or on order, for several of their future model years. G.M. adopted the internal expanding brakes also, but kept them for just the front wheels only. The internal expanding type of brake was better because the brake shoes expanded on the inside of the brake drum. The drum and lining were fully enclosed, which kept them dry, and therefore safer. The only reason General Motors kept the old exposed outside brakes for the rear wheels was that the outside brake parts were on hand, or on order, and it would have cost G.M. more money to convert to the safer, internal expanding type of brake for all four wheels. It took General Motors until the mid 1930's to even begin to use the safer hydraulic brakes.

The Model "T" Ford's brakes were discussed in the 1909 chapter, and they remained unchanged until Ford stopped making the Model "T" in May, 1927. When the Model "A" Ford was introduced for the 1928 model year, it had internal expanding mechanical brakes on all four wheels. Ford kept the unsafe mechanical brakes until past the mid 1930's.

Disc brakes were patented in 1926, yet, even now, over 60 years later, they are still not standard equipment on all four wheels, except on a very few expensive, "specialty" cars.

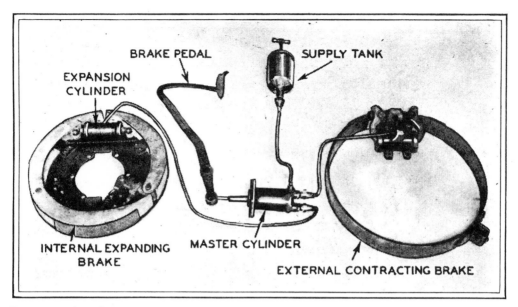

Figure 1. This photograph illustrates the layout of the hydraulic braking system. Pressure on the brake pedal forces fluid from the master cylinder to the expansion cylinders which actuate the brakes. For illustrative purposes both the internal expanding and the external contracting types are shown.

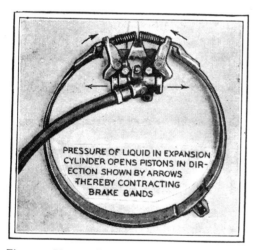

Figure 2. Here is illustrated the external contracting type of brake. Fluid hose from master cylinder is shown leading to the brake cylinder.

Early Hydraulic Brake Systems

The external contracting brake system had all the parts exposed whether hydraulic or mechanical. The lining was on the inside of the band and contracted on the outside of the brake drum (the brake drum is not shown). The internal expanding system had all the parts enclosed. The lining was on the outside of the shoes and contacted the inside of the brake drum (the brake drum is not shown).

Standardizing The Gearshift

Today, we take the gearshift for granted, especially since Ralph Nader had the government require that all automatic gearshift patterns be the same. In the 1920's, the four best selling cars in this country, Ford, Chevrolet, Buick, and Dodge Brothers, each had a different gearshift. Chevrolet was the only one to have the "standard", or S.A.E. pattern, as suggested by the Society of Automotive Engineers. The Model "T" Ford still used the pedals to shift gears; the other three all used a stick, in the middle of the floor, and a clutch pedal. All three used the "H" pattern with three speeds forward and one reverse.

The Buick and Dodge Brothers patterns were exactly opposite. With the Dodge Brothers pattern, high gear was up against the dash board. Those unfamiliar with the Dodge Brothers shift pattern were in for a surprise if they put the stick in what would be "Low" on the S.A.E. pattern, because that was reverse on the Dodge.

CHEVROLET	BUICK	DODGE BROTHERS
(S.A.E. standard)		
reverse X X second	second X X *reverse*	low X X high
low X X high	high X X low	*reverse* X X second

By the late 1920's all had changed to the S.A.E. standard shift pattern. Ford was the last to change and did so with the introduction of the Model "A" for 1928.

No Clash Shifting

Cadillac was the first to introduce no clash shifting. This consisted of a set of synchronizers inside the transmission, to get the speed of the gears to revolve at the same speed as the engine flywheel, thus avoiding the gears revolving at different speeds, which caused them to clash when shifted. Until then, it was possible to achieve this result only by "double clutching", which worked only some of the time. This was such a welcome improvement in gear shifting that, within a very few years, all manufacturers were offering it in some form or another, even on their low priced cars. Cadillac advertised this as the most important improvement for driving ease, since the advent of the self starter fifteen years earlier.

Windshield Wipers

As cars began to go a little faster, with fifty miles an hour not unusual in the late 1920's, with roads beginning to show improvement, and with more people driving during bad weather due to the popularity of the enclosed car, three other innovations were introduced as accessories. None of these had a direct influence on the other, but they are all things we now take for granted. They were the automatic windshield wiper, the automatic rear signal, or stop light, and the hydraulic shock absorber.

In earlier years, it was not unusual for the open touring car or roadster to have no windshield wiper at all. In bad weather, the driver simply pushed out the top half of the windshield so he could see straight out. The cars, themselves, could not go fast enough on the bad roads of the teens and earlier to cause very much rain or snow to blow back into the car.

Hand operated windshield wipers were available from auto accessory stores, which required that a hole be drilled through the upper frame of the windshield. When the crank lever was moved back and forth manually on the inside of the car, the blade would clean a small area directly in front of the driver's eyes on the outside of the windshield. Since the

Stop Lights

Top drawing for Goodrich tires in 1924 is a typical arrangement of the day for cars with disc wheels.

The center drawing shows the small half-moon stop light on top of a round tail light of a 1926 Oldsmobile. Because the fixture was recessed inside the spare tire rim, it was almost impossible to see either the tail light or the stop light unless you were almost directly behind the car.

Lower drawing shows stop and tail light fixture the way it was mounted on the 1930 Hupmobile's left rear fender, where it was much easier to see in heavy traffic.

The first windshield wipers were this crude type which worked by hand, as shown, and cleared a small area in front of the driver's eyes. Illustration is of a typical touring car of the mid teens to the mid 1920's era.

"RAIN-E-DAY"

WINDSHIELD CLEANER
PATENT PENDING

 PRICE $2⁰⁰

DON'T LET RAIN OR SNOW BOTHER YOU.
One turn of the handle

Clears Glass on BOTH SIDES

No other cleaner like the "RAIN-E-DAY." WHY?—IT'S THE SHAPE OF THE RUBBERS IN THE WIPERS. Cannot get out of order—always ready for use. No rattling—no scratching. FITS ANY CAR—on open cars clamps to Windshield frame—on closed cars attaches through the *frame.* If your dealer can't supply you, send us his name, with $2.00, also make of car, and we will send you, prepaid, with OUR MONEY BACK GUARANTEE if not satisfactory within ten days.

"RAIN-E-DAY" MFG. CO., 617 Pine St., SEATTLE, WASH.

driver also had to use his hands to steer and operate the spark lever, and to shift gears, (or in the case of the Model "T" Ford manually operate the gas lever instead of the gearshift) cranking the windshield wiper back and forth added to the adventures of motoring during bad weather. Making the hand windshield wiper standard equipment took many years.

The first type of windshield wiper was vacuum operated from the excess engine vacuum. This meant that the wipers would work only when the engine was running smoothly, and at a steady speed. When one would accelerate to go up a hill, the engine vacuum would drop, and the wipers would stop, then the driver would have to let up on the accelerator just long enough for the vacuum to be restored for a few seconds, so that the wipers could make another swipe or two, and the driver could see where he was going for an instant. To further complicate the operation of the automatic windshield wiper, the gasoline feed system was vacuum operated on millions of cars, so that the driver had to be careful to make sure to let up on the accelerator often enough to let the vacuum operate the wipers, as well as to let the gasoline feed system keep the engine running.

In the late 1920's electric wiper motors were installed on several brands of cars which meant that windshield wipers could now run independently of the engine vacuum. Although electrically operated windshield wipers were an improvement in their efficiency, for they would not slow down or stop at a crucial moment, they had a tendency to wear out faster and were much more expensive than the vacuum type.

Hydraulic Shock Absorbers

Until World War I, the hydraulic shock absorber was unknown in this country. It was actually developed by the French "Houdaille" people. The first large scale application of this hydraulic principle was the field artillery pieces of the French Army. When a big gun was fired, the barrel would be forced back by the explosion, then it would be brought back into firing position again by the valves opening and closing under sealed hydraulic pressure. The big gun carriage remained stationary and did not have to be aimed before being loaded and fired again. This meant that the gun could be fired again much more quickly. Before this, the force of the explosion of the shell being fired would make the gun carriage jump up off the ground. Since the gun carriage didn't come back down in exactly the same spot, it would have to be re-aimed before being fired again.

The same basic principle was applied to automobile shock absorbers, which were usually bolted to the car frame, then a lever was attached to the axle where it met the car spring. Today, hydraulic shock absorbers are tubular in shape and have been considerably improved and refined, but the principle is the same; the force of a bump causing the valves inside the hydraulic shock absorber to open and close under sealed hydraulic pressure. Ford made hydraulic shock absorbers standard equipment for the 1928 Model "A"; Chevrolet did not make them standard equipment for another couple of years.

Prior to hydraulic shock absorbers, there were "friction" shock absorbers and also the compressed air type. The friction type was made in many sizes by many manufacturers for all size cars. The compressed air type was only seen on big cars, which normally had an engine driven air compressor tire pump as standard equipment. Those air shock absorbers were very big and awkward and consisted of a large tank at each wheel, plus the necessary piping. The principle of operation was somewhat like that of the hydraulic type but compressed air was not nearly as smooth in operation as compressed hydraulic oil. Compressed air shock absorbers were not seen on new cars after the mid 1920's, when hydraulic shock absorbers were found to be superior in riding comfort and did not require those big ugly air tanks near each wheel.

One of the most popular hydraulic shock absorbers all during the 1920's and into the 1930's on some cars. Shock absorber is bolted to the car frame and a system of levers connects it to the axle at the point where the axle is bolted to the spring. Illustration shows a typical front axle installation; rear setup was almost identical.

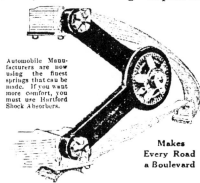
Friction Type Shock Absorbers

The shock absorber of the World War I era was known as the friction type. The drawing shows installation on a non-Ford rear spring. Front mounting would have been almost identical.

Hartford was one of the better known brands. The developer, E. V. Hartford, was a brother to the Hartford's who founded "The Great Atlantic and Pacific Tea and Spice Company", better known as the A & P grocery store.

Because of the spring suspension system on the Model "T" Ford, it could only use a shock absorber of a very limited design. The diagram shows front axle installation, but rear was almost identical. These were quite popular with Ford owners. Shock absorbers were supposed to keep the wheels from bouncing so much, therefore making the tires last longer as well as giving the passengers a smoother ride. This appeared three months before World War I ended to explain the implication of war's making prices higher. Only one tire in the drawing is shown having any tread.

Source: *National Auto History Collection
of the Detroit Public Library*

1931 Studebaker

An engine made by Studebaker was in one of the race cars at the Indianapolis 500 in 1931. Studebaker engineers made a tremendous breakthrough in engine-bearing design for their 1931 models. All their cars had this engine-bearing design including the "Indy" racer. The basic design has since been copied by every other car maker.

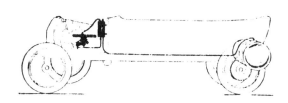

Vacuum tank system as installed on a touring car.

Cutaway view of a vacuum tank . . . . .

Closeup view of underhood installation

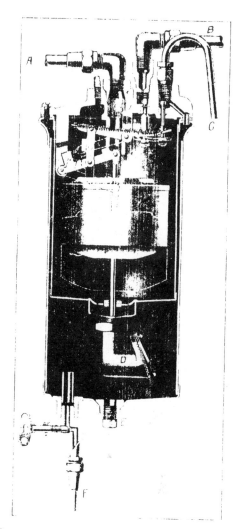

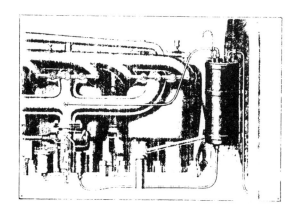

Vacuum Tank System

This schematic view shows how the basic system worked on a typical touring car of the teens and 1920's. The engine's intake manifold used the otherwise wasted engine vacuum. A pipe is used to bring the vacuum to the tank mounted high on the firewall. The tank held about a quart of gasoline; the gasoline flowed by gravity down to the carburetor. The vacuum fuel-feed system was sufficient for updraft carburetors as used on slow speed engines. They did not deliver enough gas for the downdraft carburetors of more modern high speed engines.

The underhood view shows in more detail how the system looked on a typical installation. Cutaway view shows the inner working parts. Pipe "A" brought vacuum from the engine's manifold. Pipe "B" brought the gasoline from the big tank at the rear of the car. Pipe "C" was a vent to stabilize pressure in the system. Pipe "F" allowed the gasoline flow to the carburetor. A handle could be turned to shut off the gasoline supply to the carburetor. "E" was a drain plug which could be removed to allow water to be drained from the vacuum tank.

1926 Pontiac

The Pontiac was originally made as a low-priced "companion" car to G.M.'s Oakland, falling in the price range between Chevrolet and Oakland. The Pontiac was the first car to have a mechanical fuel pump run directly off the engine's camshaft, doing away with the drawbacks of the vacuum or pressure or gravity fuel feed systems. Pontiac was the only one of G.M.'s companion cars to eventually survive while the major brand name, in Pontiac's case, Oakland, was dropped. The Olds VIKING; the Buick MARQUETTE; and the Cadillac LaSALLE were the others. Companion cars were lower-priced names sold through each of the major brand dealers to give the G.M. dealers another brand of car, lower in price, to offer.

The Mechanical Fuel Pump

Something else that we have taken for granted for many years is the mechanical fuel pump, first introduced on the 1926 Pontiac, the year of the first Pontiac. The fuel injection technology of the 1980's plus overhead cam shaft engine designs and transverse mounted engines are all reasons that the auto manufacturers are phasing in the electric fuel pump, mounted inside the gas tank. The mechanical fuel pump has been the method of obtaining the flow of gasoline in the rear of the car up to the carburetor, where it is fed into the engine. Prior to that time, gasoline arrived at the carburetor by either a pressure, or a vacuum, or a gravity system. The gravity system was the cheapest to build and Ford and a few other manufacturers merely put the gas tank in front of the car so that it was higher than the carburetor. The vacuum system had a little tank on the firewall, which was always supposed to be filled with gasoline, and which then flowed by gravity to the bowl of the updraft-style carburetor. All three of these earlier systems were poor at best and were prone to leak. Vacuum and pressure systems had to remain air tight, as well as fuel tight; and with the gravity system, the fuller the tank, the more the gas was likely to leak. Furthermore, if the little needle valve in the carburetor was faulty, the gas would also leak out.

The mechanical fuel pump system did not maintain any pressure in the lines when the engine was not running. The fuel pump runs off the camshaft of the engine and the faster the engine runs, the more fuel is required, so that being driven by the speed of the engine itself, the fuel pump runs faster and keeps up with the engine's need for fuel. Since there is a definite limit to the amount of gasoline that can be delivered by either pressure, or vacuum, or gravity systems, the introduction of the mechanical fuel pump was immediately recognized as a major improvement in the fuel system as ways of making engines faster and more efficient and powerful could be developed more freely.

In the early 1930's, it was discovered that two separate pumps could both be operated by one lever connected to the engine camshaft and both pump units could be contained in one housing. The lower unit pumped gasoline to the carburetor, while the upper unit pumped vacuum to furnish an adequate and steady supply for the windshield wipers to function without hesitating while going up a hill. One lever, in the middle of the housing, operated both pumps at the same time. Eventually, much better electric wiper motors were developed and electric wiper motors became standard equipment in the mid 1950's.

The Demise of the Independent Auto Manufacturers

Potential Auto Market Sill Not Saturated

A combination of things took place in the late 1920's and early 1930's which had been briefly described earlier. There came the demise of the small, independent auto manufacturer and the expansion of the big firms.

The saturation point had still not been reached in terms of everyone's owning a car who wanted one. This condition of the potential car market was true at the turn of the century and still true in the late 1920's, although millions of cars had been produced. This is a law of the human condition as much as anything else that only when we achieve an objective, do we recognize its limitations. At the turn of the century those who could afford a horseless carriage got a slight taste of achieving independence assumed to be attached to car ownership, but it was soon recognized that car ownership was limited by the poor roads of the time, the uncertain dependability of the vehicles available, the lack of experienced people to repair these vehicles, and the lack of easy availability of repair parts. Furthermore the top speed of the vehicles just after the turn of the century was just about 35 miles an hour.

To indicate how the potentials of the car market were still a good bit untapped in the mid and late 1920's, both General Motors and Chrysler Corp. covered every phase of the automobile price range. General Motors was just getting firmly on its financial feet and the Chrysler Corporation was new and confident. Both corporations had cars for sale from the very lowest to the very highest price ranges. General Motors had "companion" cars to their well known brands enabling G.M. dealers to have a greater price range in the lower category to offer a customer. Cadillac dealers had the lower priced "LaSalle", whose name lasted longer than any of the G.M. "companion" cars of this period. Buick had the lower priced "Marquette", Oldsmobile had the "Viking" for its low-priced car. Oldsmobile was not an excellent car in the late 1920's and the "Viking" didn't help matters at all. The Buick "Marquette" and the Oldsmobile "Viking" were dropped after only a couple of years on the market.

Oakland's "companion" car was the lower-priced "Pontiac". For several years, the Oakland had suffered from engine problems, and after about five years, the more expensive Oakland, with its bad reputation, was dropped in favor of the lower-priced "Pontiac".

The Chrysler Corporation bought the Dodge Brothers company in 1928 from the bankers who had owned it for three years, and was able to re-shuffle models and brand names. Prior to that, all Chrysler Corporation cars had been named Chrysler. Now, only the expensive cars were called Chrysler and the cheapest were called Plymouth. The newly acquired Dodge was kept in pretty much the same price range, or slightly above Plymouth, and the new DeSoto was to go between Dodge and Chrysler prices. Mr. Chrysler bought the Dodge Brothers company in the Summer of 1928, and by that autumn, DeSoto, and Plymouth, and Dodge, were all familiar products of the Chrysler Corporation.

The Ford Motor Co., still owned and controlled by Henry Ford, still stuck to the idea of building only a cheap car. The Ford company also built the Lincoln, but in very small quantities compared to the Ford. The Lincoln's price and quality put it definitely in the upper price class. It wasn't until the late 1930's that those in the Ford Motor Co. were able to convince the then aging Henry Ford to produce a medium-priced car with a new name (Mercury) as well as Ford and Lincoln.

Some of the independents had lower-priced "companion" cars too. Hudson had its Essex from 1919 until the early 1930's, when the name was changed to Essex-Terraplane for a couple of years; then just the name Terraplane was used until the late 1930's. The "Hudson" always remained the higher priced car and always kept the name Hudson.

Nash had its Ajax for a short time; Studebaker had its Erskine, and also its Rockne, each for only a few years; and several other car makers, whose names are no longer household words, also followed the pattern. Packard built a lower-priced car for several years during the 1930's, but always called it Packard, unlike Cadillac who called their lower-priced car by another name, LaSalle. It was during that time the Cadillac and Packard became equal competitors.

Henry Ford called his lower priced Lincoln the Lincoln-Zephyr, but the Lincoln-Zephyr design and engineering did not approach the quality of the LaSalle or the low-priced Packard.

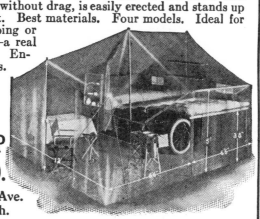
For those who preferred to use a trailer to transport their camping equipment, this company provided this compact unit. Phantom drawing shows how roomy it was when the tent was pitched. The trailer was unhooked from the car, and the car could be used for errands without disturbing the camp.

212

Pullman
Camping
Touring
Coach

A de luxe home on wheels. Low, pleasing appearance. Full head-room. Equipment includes berths, drop-leaf table, wardrobe, ice box, lockers, porcelain sink, running water, electric lights, etc.

*Write for Free Book
on Camping Vehicles.*

ZAGELMEYER AUTO CAMP CO.
906 South Henry St. **Bay City, Mich.**

Camping was becoming an ideal way for many families to spend their vacation time together in the 1920's. This coach might be considered an early motor home.

**Auto
Camping
Equipment**

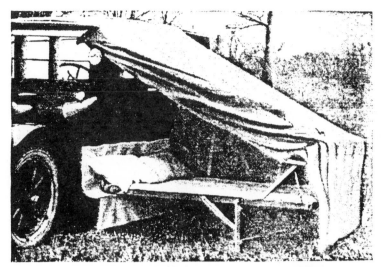

ONE NIGHT STOP

For a Longer Stay

The same Outfit is shown set up separate from the car. A perfect bed with Schilling's Famous Combination Spring Mattress Fabric.

Highest quality water and mildew proof, convertible tent.

Most available head room ever built into a tent. Entirely new.

IT IS THE 1926

Schilling
Auto - Camp

"The Quick and Easy Way"

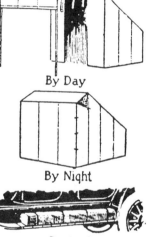

By Day

By Night

Packed

Learn About Our
New Big TOURING TRUNKS

Write for our new Catalog showing many exclusive **and** novel Touring accessories. From Factory to User.

Dept. E. **L. F. SCHILLING CO., Salem, Ohio**

An extremely compact unit for really roughing it. Despite the lower drawings showing it free standing, appears to need the car itself for support to achieve any kind of stability. It is hard to imagine that this could be folded up so completely as to fit on the running board as the illustration indicates.

Road Improvement, 1917 Style

The car is a 1913-14 Model "T" Ford. No provision was made for carrying spare tires, so the easiest place for them was on the left running board, tied to the windshield post. Ford did not provide a door for the driver; he had to use the right front door, which he left open when this photo was taken. Two spare tires were necessary because the Ford used two different size tires. Front tire size was 30 x 3 which was 24" in diameter; rear tire size was 30 x 3 1/2 which was 23" in diameter.

Concrete Roads and Gasoline

11.78 miles per gallon of gasoline on this concrete road. This is over double the mileage obtained on the earth road opposite.

5.78 miles per gallon of gasoline on this earth road—less than half the mileage obtained on the concrete road opposite.

Why Spend $2—$1 Will Do

8.49 Gallons OF GASOLINE Needed For 100 MILE RUN on the Above CONCRETE ROAD with loaded Two Ton Truck Cost at 25¢ $2.12

Tests made last September at Cleveland, O., with five 2-ton White Trucks carrying full load, showed that on an earth road in fair condition, gasoline consumption was twice that on a concrete road.

The diagrams to the left and right illustrate the relative quantities of gasoline and its cost, used by one truck in making a 100-mile run under the same condition of load over the two roads pictured above. Think what 5,000,000 motor vehicles would save in gasoline alone if they always traveled on concrete.

Since one gallon of gasoline will carry you twice as far on a concrete road as it will on an earth road, why waste the other gallon?

You pay the price of good roads whether you get them or not, and if you pay for **concrete roads** they **pay you back.**

Let's Stop This Waste!

Illinois, Pennsylvania and Michigan have voted big, road bond issues to do away with the mud tax. Many other states and counties are going to do the same thing.

When You Think of Roads—Think of Concrete;   When You Ride—Ride on Concrete

Write our nearest District Office for free copy of *"Concrete Pavements Pay for Themselves"* and *"Facts About Concrete Roads."*

PORTLAND CEMENT ASSOCIATION

OFFICES AT

ATLANTA	DENVER	HELENA	MILWAUKEE	PARKERSBURG	SEATTLE
CHICAGO	DES MOINES	INDIANAPOLIS	MINNEAPOLIS	PITTSBURGH	ST. LOUIS
DALLAS	DETROIT	KANSAS CITY	NEW YORK	SALT LAKE CITY	WASHINGTON

PAVE THE ROAD—DOUBLE THE LOAD

17.30 Gallons OF GASOLINE Needed For 100 MILE RUN on the Above Earth Road With Loaded Two Ton Truck Cost at 25¢ $4.33

This ad appeared in 1919 just after World War I ended. Good roads had saved Paris from falling to the Axis Powers during the war. Several centuries earlier the conquering Romans had built an excellent road system all throughout Europe.

The United States was desperate for good roads. This Portland Cement Co. ad tells how a smooth concrete road gives twice the gas mileage that a dirt road gives. Gas was 25 cents a gallon.

Politics Gets Into Highway Design And Routes

Better roads have always been the need of this country, and still are, for that matter. Various inducements were offered, and laws passed, primarily the Kahn-Wadsworth bill, to encourage and assist states, counties, and cities to build more roads and to improve those already in existence. After World War I, the military had large numbers of surplus heavy trucks, which this bill made available to states and municipalities at very low prices to encourage road building. The Nash Quad trucks were excellent for this work. There were other very good trucks available too, but they didn't have the four-wheel drive, and four-wheel brakes, and four-wheel steering of the Nash Quad's.

A rather unfortunate side effect was that many local minor politicians got greedy and saw to it, sometimes legally and sometimes not legally, that main roads were brought through their town. They had the idea that a tourist, passing through town, would stop and spend money in the town. What the politicians did not realize was that this idea caused more problems than it cured, for the tourists still spent the majority of their money in the big cities, unless they broke down in the small town, and the tourists also caused traffic jams to the extent that local residents were inconvenienced. By the time the mistake was realized, however, the road had already been built and in use a couple of years.

It wasn't until the design of the interstate system was adopted in the late 1950's that efficient roads were designed and engineered on a nationwide basis for the use of the traveler. The Pennsylvania Turnpike was a good example of a "limited access" highway for its time. It was opened in the late 1930's and generally followed a route across the state that a railroad had originally planned, before it ran out of money. The Turnpike was made a toll road when it first opened, and the tolls helped the State of Pennsylvania get reimbursed for the cost of the road building and for its maintenance by those who drove on it.

The Freeway system of California is another good example of a "limited access" highway and how it could be made to work very well on a very large scale, if well designed.

Better Roads Role In Improving Future Car Designs

About as many fine old names of cars which are no longer househole words went out of business in the mid 1920's as did during the later depression years of the early 1930's. This tends to underline the fact that the depression, as such, in itself, was not the cause of the independents going under. Better roads were one of the major, although indirect causes. As roads improved and credit became easier to obtain, more people bought cars and traveled. The larger automobile corporations had a larger network of dealers, with repair facilities and stocks of parts. The smaller, independent auto manufacturers did not have this advantage. Furthermore, if a car needed repair in a small town, one was more likely to find a mechanic who knew how to fix a well-known brand of car than one of the independent makes, simply because there were more of the well-known brands on the road to give the repair shop mechanic experience in repairing them. The same was true with replacement parts. The drivers, or the mechanic fixing the car, were more likely to find a replacement part for a well-known brand of car than for one of the independent makes.

As roads became more heavily traveled, the public, away from home, soon learned which cars were easily repaired by a mechanic on the road, and which cars were not. They also learned which cars gave the most problems, and this is where good roads played such an important part. Since roads were being built in the mid 1920's which could be traveled at 60 miles an hour, the public wanted to be able to drive at the rate of 60 miles an hour. It was soon discovered which cars would withstand that kind of driving, and which would not be able to hold up.

Source: *National Auto History Collection
of the Detroit Public Library*

1929 Jordans In Showroom

The Jordan was another "assembled" car; it was still being assembled as late as 1929 as evidenced in this showroom photo.

Note the 1928-29 Model "A" Ford two-door parked outside at the curb, with the one-piece windshield fully opened for ventilation.

As an example, the Model "T" Ford had a top speed of 40 to 45 miles an hour under ideal conditions. If the Model "T" were an enclosed car, the additional weight and wind resistance of the body brought the top speed down to about 35 miles an hour. People were no longer satisfied with driving at those lower speeds on the open highway. The result was that the public stopped buying the Model "T" Ford mainly because the Model "T" would not go fast enough. It took Henry Ford several years to realize this fact and to change to production of the faster Model "A" Ford for the 1928 model year. Times had been changing so fast, however, that the Model "A" Ford was already so much out of date by the time it was introduced that it was taken off the market after only four years!

Each and every car manufacturer had to go through a modernization process. While the example above was given of Ford, all other manufacturers had to do exactly the same thing. Some had realized this before Henry Ford and had gone ahead earlier and they survived. Walter P. Chrysler was one of these and even his pet, the "Chrysler Six", was modernized after being on the market for just two years. The Old Maxwell, which became the Chrysler Four, then the Chrysler 58, and then the Plymouth, was extensively modernized by 1928. One of the main reasons Chrysler bought the Dodge company was because it had just modernized its cars, dropping their old slow speed four-cylinder engine, and modernizing the chassis as well, to include hydraulic brakes, a new six-cylinder engine, a modern gear shift, a two unit electrical system, and other improvements.

During the 1920's the development of vastly improved gasoline, in addition to "ethyl" or premium, made existing cars run very much better. But more important, it allowed, and even encouraged development of higher compression engines, with more refined ignition systems, and more refined carburetion and manifold systems.

Why "Franklin" And "Willys-Knight" Failed

We will mention just two of the independent manufacturers who did not modernize and how it meant their demise. Their names are no longer household words to many people any more, but the engines each of them built were quite different from other engines. Their mistakes were in trying to modernize their particular types of slow speed engines. The Franklin and Willys-Knight engines must each be described separately, here.

The Air Cooled Franklin, A Failure

The Franklin was air cooled, meaning that it did not have a radiator and a liquid (water) to run through the engine to keep the engine at an efficient operating temperature. Instead, the Franklin had cooling fins sticking out of the outside of the cylinders, to dissipate the heat generated by the engine. The Franklin also used a blower fan and sheet metal duct work, to force the air across and over the cooling fins. There had been other cars with air-cooled engines on the market from time to time, but Franklin was the oldest and best known, with the best air cooled engine of its day.

In more modern times the Chevrolet Corvair of the 1960's was air-cooled, also the same decade saw many Volkswagens imported into this country. Both the Corvair and the Volkswagen of that period were downright unsafe because of their rear engine chassis design, but their air-cooled engine trouble is the main reason both are now considered oddities when they are seen on the streets. The Corvair engine was the "opposed" type with six cylinders; the V.W. was the same type with four cylinders.

The Franklin had evolved from four cylinders to six through the years, but they were always the "in line" type, as were most of the fours and sixes of their era. There is nothing

Horse Collar Franklin

Because of the shape of the front air intake, made to resemble the hood of other cars, this model (1923) Franklin was nicknamed the "horse collar". It was at this time that they should have dropped the air-cooling idea. Note that the front license tag is off to the side, so it does not block air flowing through the air intake. The model immediately preceding the "horse collar" Franklin was the "shovel nose" Franklin.

Source: National Auto History Collection
of the Detroit Public Library

Franklin Cooling System

This is how it looked when the right side of the hood was raised on a Franklin of the early 1930's. The big round object on the right was the duct work around the "squirrel cage" type blower or fan. The blower was attached to the front of the engine's crankshaft. Air was drawn in by the blower, then blown across and down over the engine parts, through all the duct work shown here. The six wire loops on top of the engine were spring clips to hold the valve covers in place. Unlike liquid cooled engines, air cooled engines have individual cylinders, cylinder heads, and valve covers.

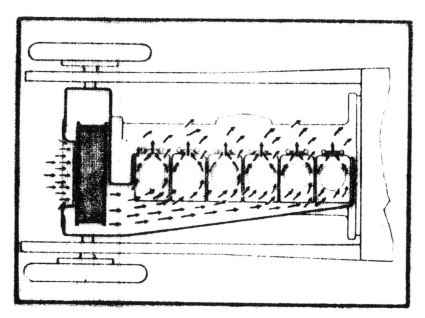

*Air is forced under high pressure through-
out the Franklin engine, allowing the
exact amount needed for each part.*

Top view of the air flow pattern for the Franklin cooling system.

1933 Franklin Olympic

They stuck with their same basic air-cooled engine design and that was their downfall. By 1933, this was an "assembled" car except for the engine. Bodies were bought from Reo, lights from Guide, engine electrical parts from Delco-Remy, brakes, transmissions, etc. were from other manufacturers. The year after this Franklin was made, the company went bankrupt.

Forced in by the air-turbine fan, the air is carried in enormous volume over the tops of the cylinders — down through the cooling flanges which surround each cylinder — with greater amounts alloted to points of greater heat.

Franklin Cooling System

Phantom drawing showing how air was sucked in through the blower on the front of the Franklin engine and forced through the sheet metal duct work over the engine parts. It worked reasonably well at slow speeds only.

wrong with the basic principle of air cooling, providing it is done under the right circumstances. The Franklin people had it down to an exact science. Their mistake was when they tried to make the car go too fast. The result was that the engine overheated, because the higher the speed of the engine the more heat it generated, which could not be dissipated quickly enough. This is also basically what happened to the Corvair and V.W. engines, when these cars were redesigned to make the engines run faster so that the cars would travel faster.

Airplane engines do not have exactly the same situation as automobiles. They are not placed under the same type of hood as a car; they are also the "radial" type, which means that the cylinders form a circle. Some light planes have the "opposed" type engine, but which ever type the air plane has, the design of the plane is such that the cylinders stick out where they are exposed to all the air that the propeller moves back across them. It is true that an airplane engine runs at higher speeds than an automobile engine; it is also true that the explosions of the fuel inside are hotter in an airplane engine than in an air-cooled automobile engine. However, the ratio of heat generated to horsepower produced is not the same. While it revolves faster and runs hotter, the radial engine used in small airplanes has always been more efficient because of its radial design which permits more surface area to be air-cooled. The way it is able to be installed in an airplane, with unrestricted air flowing over it, cannot be duplicated in a land vehicle which would have the road close to the lower portion of the engine and other vehicles close to the sides.

Sleeve Valves In The Knight Engine, A Failure

The Knight engine was only one of the engine design types used by the Willys-Overland Co. of Toledo, and Willys-Knight was their highest priced car. It was liquid (water) cooled, but the Knight engine had a very different arrangement of valves from any other engine. It had "sleeve" valves; other cars have "poppet" valves, because the valves pop up and down at high speeds. The sleeves of the Knight engine moved up and down also. The piston traveled inside one sleeve, and that sleeve traveled up and down inside a second sleeve. Near the top of each sleeve was a little hole, and there was another hole just opposite the first hole, but at a fraction of an inch higher or lower. At just the right instant, the two holes in each sleeve would line up, and a charge of air and fuel would come through the combined opening into the cylinder. Then, as the piston would move up to compress the charge, the sleeves would move so that the holes no longer lined up, forming a seal to eliminate a compression leak. After the explosion of the compressed air and fuel had taken place, and the piston was driven down to actually do the work, the two holes in the sleeves on the opposite sides of the cylinders would line up and the exhaust gasses would be driven out. Then the first holes would move so that they would not be lined up, and the entire process would be repeated.

Until oil became improved it contained a lot of carbon, which would tend to stop things up to a great extent in a regular engine. The carbon content of the early oil refining process actually helped the Knight engine, however, as the seals between the sleeves and the pistons became loaded with carbon to form a better seal, which made the engine run better as it got older. Then came better oil and better roads and faster car speeds.

The sleeves were operated up and down by miniature connecting rods on a miniature crankshaft, which would correspond to the cam shaft in a regular engine. The sleeves, however, were too big and awkward to move at extremely high speeds. The result was that the sleeves would break at the point of their greatest stress, which was where they were attached to the connecting rods. Willys discontinued the Knight engine in 1932, because of this problem, then concentrated on very small cars, which it has made ever since, however the Daimler cars in England continued using the Knight engine until 1939.

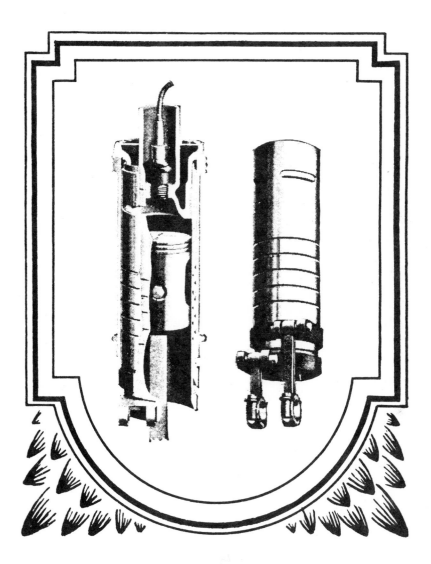

Knight Engine Principle

Phanton drawing shows the piston inside the one sleeve, and that sleeve inside a second sleeve, and openings which are lined up to admit air and fuel or expel exhaust fumes. Other drawing shows the method of making sleeves move up and down by using small connecting rods. The sleeves could not move up and down fast enough at high speed, so they would break at their weakest point which is where they were attached to the small connecting rod. When a sleeve broke, the entire engine would be damaged beyond repair in just one or two revolutions, which was before it could be shut off by the driver. Illustration is of a Willys-Knight, but all cars with the "Knight" engine were based on the same principle.

1931 Willys-Knight

The day of the Knight was just about over. The last domestic car with a Knight engine was made in 1932 by Willys and was almost identical to the one shown here. In 1929, Stearns-Knight, of Cleveland, was just about to stop production of all Stearns and Knight operations, which allowed Willys to be the sole producers of Knight engine cars in this country through 1932. Starting in 1933, Willys made only very small cars with regular engines. The four-cylinder engine that they started producing in 1933 was kept and modified and became the basic Jeep engine during World War II.

The Oakland V-8 Becomes The Pontiac V-8

In 1929 Oakland came out with a V-8 engine. Several expensive cars had V-8's and Packard had a V-12 at one time. The Oakland V-8 was a breakthrough, in that the engine block and crankcase were all together of one casting. Until then, the crankcase, or lowerhalf of the engine, was separate and bolted to the cylinder black, or upperhalf of the engine. A few years later, in 1932, Ford brought out its low priced V-8, and it, too, had a one piece casting, as do all engines today.

The last Oakland automobile was manufactured in 1931, but since the company had a lot of V-8 engines already built, the 1932 Pontiac was a V-8. In 1933 Pontiac came out with its straight-eight engine which it kept for over twenty years, modifying and improving it from time to time, until it returned to a V-8 again in 1955. Pontiac also made a six-cylinder engine during those years.

The 1930's

Cars Become More Comfortable And Dependable

By the end of the 1930's, a good number of technical advances had been made. All cars had hydraulic brakes; safety glass was also standard. It was unusual, but not unheard of, for the lowest priced cars to be built with only one taillight, one windshield wiper, and one sun visor.

While still requiring almost as much maintenance as previously, cars were becoming more comfortable and dependable. More cars were having heaters, defrosters, and radios installed and turn signals were just becoming available. The expensive Packard even had "factory" air conditioning, which they advertised as "mechanical refrigeration", available, as did Cadillac and the big Chrysler just prior to World War II.

The Weird Looking Airflow

For 1934, Chrysler gave the public a treat, the Airflow! Chrysler also made a slightly less expensive version of the Airflow for the DeSoto. Although the looks of the Airflow were downright weird, the design and innovations were tremendous in most ways. Those people who could be talked into taking a test drive in the Airflow usually bought one because of the superior ride and handling. The appearance was so radical that all Chrysler could do with it the following year was to give the Airflow a facelift.

Apparently the novelty of the design wore off, as 1936 was the last year for the DeSoto Airflow and 1937 was the last year for the Chrysler Airflow. However, during the Airflow years, Chrysler and DeSoto had wisely continued their normal looking cars, which were called Air*stream*. Chrysler also made sure that the engineering advantages were put into the Airstream models, as well as added to the lower priced Dodge and Plymouth.

RAIN STORMS will play tricks on you. And so will an old motor—unless it has Ethyl.

But stop beside the pump that bears the Ethyl emblem every time you need gas and then you *know* what your car will do.

It will run its best all the time! You don't always want flashing pick-up—or the extra power it takes to zoom over hills in high. But when you do, you *want 'em!*

Stop at an Ethyl pump and discover what millions of others know

today: *The next best thing to a brand-new car is your present car with Ethyl.* With oil companies selling Ethyl at only 2c a gallon over the price of regular, you can't afford not to use it. The savings in repairs and upkeep more than offset this new low premium. Ethyl Gasoline Corporation, New York City.

Ethyl contains lead. © E. G. C. 1933

NOW SOLD BY OIL COMPANIES AT *only* **2**C PER GALLON *over "regular"*

This is an example of why the rumble seat lost its popularity by 1933. For just a few dollars more, the buyers could get a two door or a four door sedan where everyone sat inside.

Source: *National Auto History Collection of the Detroit Public Library*

1932 Ford V-8 Sedan

1932 was the first year for a V-8 engine in a Ford. In addition to the V-8, Ford also made a four-cylinder car in 1932, the Model "B". It looked like the V-8 in general outward appearance, but, of course, did not have "V-8" on the hub caps and on the tie bar between the headlights as the car pictured here.

230

Source: *National Auto History Collection of the Detroit Public Library*

1932 Essex Sedan

This 1932 Essex had a popular accessory of the period, a trunk. It was bolted onto the rear of the square backed body and the spare tire rim holder was bolted onto the back of the trunk. The lid was rather small and on the very top making it rather difficult to load or unload. A few years later, more streamlined bodies with built in trunks large enough to hold the spare tire inside became available. With built in trunks, the entire back of the trunk opened up, not just the top, making it much easier to load and unload.

Source: *National Auto History Collection
of the Detroit Public Library*

1937 Ford V-8 Sedan

Although these Fords with their V-8 engines were capable of 75 miles an hour, they still only had mechanical brakes and the 30 year-old spring suspension design. Hydraulic brakes came on Fords in 1938; the spring suspension design remained for over ten more years.

This was the first Ford to have a front opening (alligator) style hood. The ornament in front was rotated 90 degrees to the side to unlock the hood, then returned to its straight ahead postion after the hood was closed. The side panels, from the tops of the fenders to the bottom of the hood, could easily be unbolted after the hood was raised. That allowed side access when more extensive service was needed.

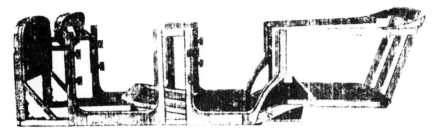

Fig. 1 An Open-Car Body Frame (Nash)

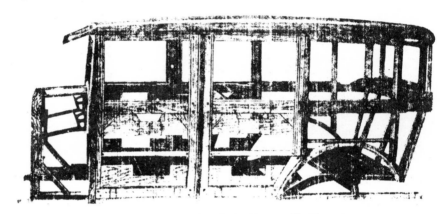

Fig. 2 A Closed-Body Car Frame (Nash)

The Wood Framed Body

Steel sheet metal panels were nailed on over the outside and upholstery was nailed on over the inside. These bodies were prone to creak and groan at inopportune times. If a car with one of these bodies was involved in a collision severe enough to break a wood part, repairs would be so expensive that the car would be a total loss unless the car was almost new. Likewise, if rot were to develop due to an unrepaired water leak, replacement of a wood part would be quite costly. All steel bodies, in addition to being much stronger, did not have the above drawbacks.

Source: *National Auto History Collection of the Detroit Public Library*

1934 Chrysler Airflow

1934 turned out to be an important year for engineering developments in this country. Chrysler introduced the Airflow which had more engineering firsts than probably any car, before or since. Chrysler and General Motors and several independent manufacturers introduced independent front wheel suspension. Dodge and Plymouth returned to straight front axles for four more years, then returned to I.F.S. for good. Chrysler and DeSoto kept I.F.S. on their Airstream models, however.

Vent windows were also introduced by Chrysler and General Motors in 1934 and several independents. Dodge and Plymouth returned to the single pane type glass for four more years, then re-introduced them and retained them for good. Chrysler and DeSoto kept the vents on their Airstream models, however.

Ford did not have I.F.S.; they retained their 25 year-old transverse spring and straight axle design and did not go to an I.F.S. arrangement for another fifteen years, until after World War II. Ford did not have vents on all their models until 1940.

234
234

Source: *National Auto History Collection
of the Detroit Public Library*

Chrysler Factory Showroom

1934 Airflow and Airstream Chryslers and DeSotos along with 1934 Plymouths on display at the large factory showroom in Detroit. One sample of every model was said to be on display here.

Source: *National Auto History Collection*
of the Detroit Public Library

Airflow Phantom

This phantom drawing shows the weight distribution, not considered very important until now. The engine was moved forward, directly over the wheel center. This helped give the passengers a smoother ride as well as making the car easier to steer.

The early (1934) Airflows had the spare tire mounted outside; later models had built in trunks with the spare inside.

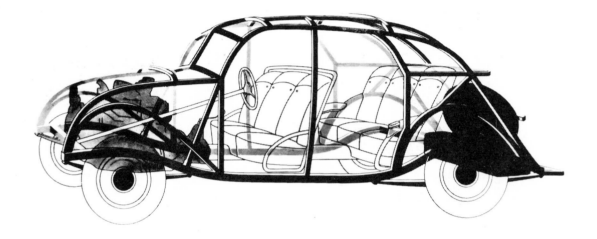

Source: *National Auto History Collection
of the Detroit Public Library*

Phantom Airflow

In the Phantom drawing highlighting the frame structure of the Airflow four-door sedan, note that the lower end of the steering column is in front of the front wheels, which allowed the steering linkage to be behind the steering gear. This gave the driver much easier steering, and more control because he did not have the force of the wheel bounce transmitted through the steering column.

The body frame structure and the steering arrangement were but two of the countless engineering firsts pioneered by the Chrysler Airflow.

Zephyr Cutaway

An actual Lincoln Zephyr body with half the outer panels not installed to allow the inner structure to be seen. As with the Airflow Chrysler and DeSoto and all other unit body construction, the steel framework is welded together to form a very strong unit; the outer panels are then welded on to add even more strength.

The gentleman with his back to the camera and the slight bald spot is waving his right hand as he explains an important feature to the potential buyers, looking on. In the mid 1930's shutter speeds on cameras were not what they are now, so candid shots like this made the gesture with the right hand appear as a blur.

THE ONLY CAR OF ITS KIND

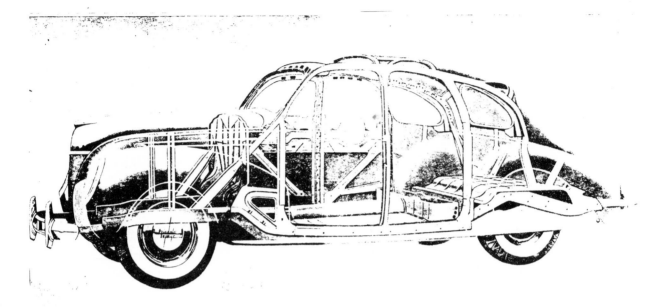

Phantom Lincoln Zephyr

The first Lincoln Zephyr appeared in 1936 and was virtually unchanged during its 13-year life except for replacing the graceful teardrop-shaped fenders, shown on this 1939 model, with the square boxy type starting in 1942. The original Lincoln Continentals were based on a modified Zephyr design.

Lincoln-Zephyr Copies The Airflow Body Idea

Lincoln paid Chrysler a big compliment by copying its unit body idea from the Airflow for its new low-priced Lincoln, the Zephyr, for 1936. It was not nearly as weird looking as the Chrysler Airflow, so the Zephyr sold much better. The Zephyr had a small V-12 engine, but it had the same transverse type spring suspension design, and mechanical brake design as the Fords of the mid 1930's. These two designs were tremendous drawbacks to ease of riding and handling.

The looks of the Lincoln-Zephyr evolved, and eventually the sleek, streamlined fenders of the mid 1930's were replaced with a bulky looking boxy type of fender. Finally, the Zephyr was given hydraulic brakes, but the spring suspension design was never modernized.

Edsel Ford, Clara and Henry's only child, had a Zephyr somewhat redesigned and customized for his own personal use, and in 1938, had it shipped to Boca Raton, Florida where he planned to spend his winter vacation. Those who saw it admired it and pestered him so much, because they wanted to buy one, that Edsel decided to start producing it. The new car was named the Lincoln Continental.

The Cadillac Sixteen

Another of Charles Kettering's famous projects was begun in the late 1920's, and was introduced on the 1930 Cadillac. This was the beginning of the most famous Cadillac series, the sixteen-cylinder engine. Had this engine first appeared on the market at any other time than at the beginning of the worst of the depression years, this sixteen-cylinder engine might have been better received. 1930 was the only good year it had.

The idea of so many cylinders is to get smoothness, as the firing of the engine overlaps to such a degree that vibration is almost nil. Full page ads were run in *Fortune Magazine* saying the number of sixteen-cylinder cars produced by Cadillac in 1933 would be limited to 400; another said the same thing for 1934. In actual fact, only between fifty and sixty cars were built for each of those years. The engine was completely changed for 1938, and the V-16 was dropped for good in 1940.

Two glaring faults stand out on the V-16 engine. One fault is their unquenchable thirst for gasoline. Tops in performance was six miles per gallon, and then only when everything was in good condition and in perfect tune. The other fault of the Cadillac V-16 was the surrendering to the stylists of the time, and having two up-draft carburetors designed through the 1937 model year, just so the car could have a particular hood design! The newer downdraft type of carburetor was much more efficient and would very likely have given more than the top mileage of six miles per gallon. Another glaring drawback of the Cadillac V-16 was its out-of-date and unsafe mechanical brakes, after even the standard Cadillacs had switched to hydraulic brakes.

In 1931 Cadillac came out with a V-12 engine, in addition to the V-16, and the old stand-by V-8. The V-12 was the same as the V-16, except that it had two fewer cylinders on each side. The V-8 was completely different in design. The last Cadillac V-12 was built in 1937.

Nash Motors Survives The Depression

Charles W. Nash resigned as President of Nash Motors in 1930 and became Chairman of the Board of Directors. Nash Motors was the most profitable automobile manufacturer in the depression year of 1932. It made over a million dollars profit, while General Motors made less than a quarter million in profit. *ALL* the other auto makers in this country lost money in

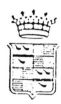

The Nineteen Thirty-three production of the

CADILLAC V·SIXTEEN

will be limited to Four Hundred Cars

custom built to order

creating an entirely new plane of fine car

ownership

This Cadillac ad implied that only 400 V-16 cars would be built in 1933; another ad said the same thing for 1934. Actually, not even 60 V-16's were built each of those two years. Possibly the ad was meant to imply that the cars were meant strictly for "THE" social elite 400.

Two Pioneers Meet Again

Ransom E. Olds, in the light suit, and Charles W. Nash meet again in the sunset of their lives at a pioneer automobile gathering in 1946.

1932, and several went under. In 1933 and 1934, however, Nash Motors *LOST* over a million dollars for each of those two years, and a little over half a million in 1935.

By 1934, Nash had made its millionth car. In 1936, Nash introduced a feature which allowed the inside of the car to be converted into a double bed; Nash kept this feature for twenty years on one model or another.

The depression was really the beginning of the end for Nash Motors, as it merged with Kelvinator in 1937. It had hopes of being as big a name in the home appliance business as Frigidaire was as a General Motors division, but it didn't turn out that way. Nash Motors was what Charles Nash wanted it to be during his active years.

Inventor's Names Given To Famous Products

Several men gave their names to various inventions which have now become household words. We have already spoken of the over running clutch which Vincent Bendix invented shortly after Kettering's invention of the self-starter. The over-running clutch is still used on starters today and it is known as a bendix drive. J. L. McAdam invented a process for paving streets, which became known as macadam, and was quite popular before the advantages of concrete were so widely known. Mr. Schrader invented a very small one-way valve to hold a considerable amount of pressure. The automobile industry has been using them in tires for many years and now in modern auto air conditioning systems. It is known as a schrader valve and you use it every time you check the air in your tires. Until recently, every time Dr. Rudolph Diesel's invention appeared in print, it was spelled with a capital "D". Now, it has become such a familiar name that a small "d" is accepted. A gentleman from Scotland gave his name to many auto and aircraft inventions of the 1920's. His name was Loughead, but he realized that we, in this country, would not pronounce his name correctly. He spelled the company's name the way he knew we could pronounce it correctly, Lockheed.

Men Using Names And Initials On Their Products

Albert Champion sold the company he named for himself, the Champion Ignition Company, whose chief product was spark plugs. Then he started another company to make spark plugs. This time he used his initials as the company's name A.C. Both concerns are still in business today and are still making spark plugs.

We have already mentioned how Ransom Eli Olds left the first company he founded, making the Oldsmobile, and formed a new company using his initials, R.E.O.

Harry A. Lozier made a medium-priced car he called the Lozier for several years. Then he arranged with the Weidley Comapny to buy their V-12 engines for his prestige car, the H.A.L. Twelve. The H.A.L. Twelve was no match for the Packard V-12 (twin six) and both Lozier and the H.A.L. Twelve were through by about 1920.

Before 1910, Harry C. Stutz designed a car with wheels that were 43 inches tall and had an underslung frame. The car was named the American Underslung. A few years later he designed the famous car with his name on it; later he left the Stutz Motor Car Company and designed another car, the name of which consisted of only his intitials, H.C.S. The H.C.S. had a tremendous resemblance to the Stutz cars which were still being made; however, the H.C.S. cars were only made a very few years.

The old size and the new size bills of the late 1920's when the old were being phased out. When the etching for the new size was made in 1928, the most popular car was included on the ten dollar bill.

The 1928 Model "A" Ford at the Treasury Building. Take a ten dollar bill from your wallet and see for yourself!

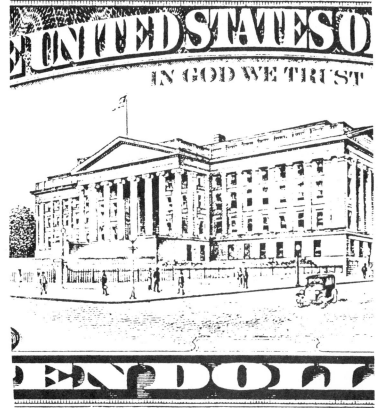

The Model "A" Ford And The Ten Dollar Bill

Another story which somewhat involves the automobile started in the mid 1920's and began to end in 1928. It seems that the "powers that be", who decide such things decided to change the size of our paper money. The size of the old money was 3-1/8" X 7-3/8". It was reduced to 2-3/4" X 6-3/8" which it remains today. Different pictures of the Presidents and of other famous men of history were selected, and new etchings of buildings were chosen for the reverse sides of the bills.

On the reverse side of the ten dollar bill, they decided to put a picture of the U.S. Treasury Building in Washington. By the left front corner of the Treasury Building, they decided to draw in a picture of a car that was the most up-to-date and talked about, popular, low-priced car of 1928, the new Model "A" Ford. As a matter of fact, you can take a ten dollar bill from your wallet right now and look at it, and you will see the 1928 Model "A" Ford at the corner of the Treasury Building. If you have a magnifying glass, the details are even more obvious. Most people don't realize that they are walking around with a picture of a 1928 Ford in their pocket.

History Now Ended

The object of this book, in so far as history of the names that are still household words is concerned, has now been achieved. Events that have taken place in the past forty or so years since World War II can easily be learned by anyone who is really interested. There are always enough retired automobile executives still living who will be glad to tell of their experiences during their active years for modern students to write that phase of history. Many have already written very interesting and entertaining books about their experiences.

The End Of The Line

As these 1942 Plymouths have reached the end of their assembly line about the time the United States entered World War II, this book has also reached the end of its line, having begun in 1895.

Later generations will continue with the history of the automobile business in this country using World War II as their starting point.

Bibliography

American Motors Family Album. Detroit: American Motors Public Relations Department, 1969.

Borth, Christy. "The Great Men Of Detroit." *True's Automobile Yearbook #9,* 1960.

Clymer, Floyd. *Henry's Wonderful Model T.* New York: Bonanza Books, 1965.

Dammann, George H. *Sevent-Five Years Of Buick.* Glen Ellyn, New York: Crestline Publishing, 1973.

_____ . *Seventy Years Of Chrysler.* Glen Ellyn, New York: Crestline Publishing, 1974.

Duerksen, Menno. "Packard, Part II." *Cars & Parts,* 1970.

_____ . "Knight and Willys," *ibid.*

_____ . "Childe Harold Wills, Part I," *ibid.*

Gustin, Lawrence R. *Billy Durant, Creator Of General Motors.* Grand Rapids, Michigan: William B. Erdmans Publishing Co., 1973.

Hendry, Maurice D. *Cadillac, The Complete Seventy Year History.* New York: Automobile Quarterly Publications, 1973.

"Henry Ford Through The Years." *Life Magazine,* 1937.

Horseless Carriage Gazette. Los Angeles, California: Horseless Carriage Club, 1966.

Marvin, Keith and Arthur Lee Homan. "The Cars of 1923." *Automobilists of the Upper Hudson Valley,* 1957.

Kimes, Beverly Rae. "Oldsmobile, The First Seventy-Five Years." *Automobile Quarterly Publications,* 1972.

McPherson, Thomas A. *The Dodge Story.* Ellyn, Illinois: Crestline Publications, 1975.

Olson, Sidney. "How The Ford Money Rolled In." *Life Magazine,* 1953.

Pinkerton, Robert E. "Ed Apperson and the Horseless Carriage." *True's Automobile Yearbook #1,* 1952.

Rae, John B. *The American Automobile.* Chicago: University of Chicago Press, 1965.

Snyder, Frank T. "Henry Ford's First Patent Suit." *Old Cars,* 1971.

Thron, L. Edward and James S. Crenshaw. *Popular Mechanics Auto Album.* New York: Popular Mechanics Press, 1952.

100 Years On The Road. South Bend, Indiana: The Studebaker Corporation, 1952.